MORE REAL FOOD RECIPES

By
Jurea L. Dawson

TEACH Services, Inc.
Brushton, New York

2007   08   09   10   11   12   ·   5   4   3   2   1

Copyright © 2007 TEACH Services, Inc.
ISBN-13: 978-1-57258-450-1
ISBN-10: 1-57258-450-5
Library of Congress Control Number: 2006933647

Published by

TEACH Services, Inc.
www.TEACHServices.com

CONTENTS

A WORD OF THANKS

Mom, I would like to thank you for teaching me the art of healthful cooking at an early age and for encouraging my creativity with food by allowing me to experiment on my own in the kitchen. Now as an adult I have a profound appreciation for food. This gift you have taught me has blessed my life and many others.

Dad, thanks for all your support and encouragement through the years. I always know if a new recipe is a success when you clean your plate!

To Danielle, my sister and my friend, we work together in the kitchen like magic! Thanks for your love, encouragement, your recipes and many culinary ideas.

Bekki, my self declared "agent," I want to thank you for believing in me and continually encouraging me to do things I never dreamed possible.

To my nephew Vernon, who stands on a stool to watch me make pancakes, you may only be two, but I can already tell you're going to love cooking!

I want to thank God for sparing my life and for giving me gifts that I can use to bless others.

INTRODUCTION

"REAL" Food Defined!

"Real" foods are fruits and vegetables, grains, nuts, seeds and legumes taken directly from nature unaltered, unrefined, unprocessed or minimally processed and prepared in a simple and healthy manner that preserves so far as possible the foods natural flavor and nutrition.

It is now widely recognized that poor diet and lifestyle are main contributors to sickness and disease. There is a popular quote that says, "You are what you eat!" The growing number of diet related diseases now thriving in our modern day civilization is proof to the truth of these words. Health is a priceless treasure. Eating healthy and developing healthy lifestyle habits is the surest way to protect one's health and wellbeing.

More Real Food Recipes is a cook book about how to take natural whole food ingredients like fruits, vegetables, grains, nuts and seeds and turn them into tasty palatable dishes that can be savored and enjoyed. In my travels I have encountered people who desire to eat healthy, but they don't know how to take simple raw ingredients and make them taste good. To many the term "health food" equals oatmeal, broccoli, and salad. Of course these foods are not excluded, but you certainly are not limited to such a scanty fare, and the many ways in which these foods can be prepared is limitless! With a little imagination simple foods can be turned into scrumptious mouth-watering meals. Eating should be a pleasurable activity. A meal eaten in drudgery is no good for the digestion. So for over twenty years my goal as a vegetarian chef has been to create healthy recipes, yet preserve the flavor of food which is so essential to its enjoyment. Healthy food with flavor, this is what *More Real Food Recipes* is all about!

Jurea L. Dawson

That's How I Remember Grandma

By Jurea L. Dawson

Grandma was a woman of kindness and affection
Born with a heart full of love and compassion.
A mother to her own, and to those who were not,
To love and to care was her God given lot
That's how I remember Grandma.

Grandma reached out to the old and the young,
With a helping hand or a loving scold.
Many found comfort in her warm embrace,
The hurt and rejected always had a place.
That's how I remember Grandma.

Grandma loved to cook with her heart and soul,
Creating miracles with pot, spoon, and bowl.
Her Eggplant Parmesan was a favorite dish,
And her barbecue sauce you just couldn't resist.
That's how I remember Grandma.

Grandma loved to hear Sandi Patty sing,
When "Upon ths Rock" played, she'd sway and sing.
Her eyes would close and her hands would raise
As she lifted her heart in a song of praise.
That's how I remember Grandma.

Grandma loved to go bargain shopping,
She'd find great deals on odds 'n ends.
She could stretch a dollar right to the max.
And at the flea market you don't pay tax.
That's how I remember Grandma.

Grandma left no money, no house or land,
But a legacy of love our hearts can understand.
A family recipe and so many memories dear,
Your love for us Grandma was shown very clear.
You will be remembered Grandma.

Though death's icy grasp has torn us apart,
There will come a day when we will never part.
When Jesus descends from the clouds in the sky,
We'll be reunited in that sweet by and by.
We'll see you again Grandma.

So goodbye Grandma, we miss you very much.
The sound of your voice, the warmth of your touch.
Our hearts are heavy and our eyes sore,
But the hope in our hearts will forever endure.
We love you Grandma.

This poem was written in memory of my Grandmother, Margaret Dawson who passed away February 20th, 2000.

My Grandmother was an inspirational cook and a master at flavor. My sisters and I learned many "tricks of the trade" from her. She was well known for her great food and loving heart.

NO TIME TO COOK!

"Impossible!" Exclaimed Jessica to her friend Rachel. "There is no way I'm going to be able to make all these healthy foods from scratch. I am much too busy to do this."

Jessica had run into her good friend Rachel while grocery shopping and they fell into a lively conversation about diet, health, and cooking natural foods.

"I know what you mean," replied Rachel. "My family and I eat out several times a week. It gets expensive, but it's the only way I can keep my sanity. I can count on one hand how many times I'm actually in the kitchen in a weeks time."

"Eating out is my life," said Jessica, " I'm a business women and I'm rarely home, and when I am home I'm too tired to think about cooking anything. I can't even remember the last time my poor husband had a home cooked meal."

"I know," said Rachel shaking her head despondently, with no apparent solutions forthcoming.

"But I really do need to change my diet. I know it's important if I 'm going to be healthy. I just don't know how to fit all this cooking into my already tight schedule," Jessica ended with a sigh.

"Well, it's been nice chatting with you Jessica," said Rachel abruptly. " I've got to finish shopping then I have to pick up my kids from school, but do let me know if you come up with an answer to this cooking dilemma."

"I will," promised Jessica. "If I ever get time," she said with a laugh.

With that the two ladies departed company, their shopping carts traveling in opposite directions.

Do you have this problem? Check out the suggestions below.

Suggestions:

Time. No one seems to have enough of it. Where does it all go? We all have the same 24 hours allotted to us each day, yet for some of us there just doesn't seem to be enough hours in a day to get everything done, especially for those things we really need to do, like eating better and taking care of ourselves.

There was a period in history when man had enough time to plant his own food, harvest it, can and stock it up for winter, plus prepare it, then start the cycle all over again the next year. And that's not all; he built his own cabin, made his own clothes, made the candles for his light, cut his own firewood for heat, and then he even had enough time to sit by his own fireside in the evening with his dog slumbering at the hearth and a good book in his hand. I've often wondered about this phenomenon. How is it that today we have more conveniences and less time for the important things in life like family, friends, and taking care of ourselves? We drive cars, ride buses and airplanes, buy our clothes and food, we use cell phones, e-mail, and fax machines for easy instant communication. We shop and pay bills on our computers online. What is eating up our time? Think about it. Maybe convenience is not the issue; maybe what we need is SIM-PLICITY! While you think about this, let me give you some suggestions on how to find more time to cook.

1. Make cooking a priority; don't make it an option, but a necessity to health. We tend to make time for the things we prioritize.

2. Select a day in the week when you can utilize several hours to make up a few casseroles to freeze. A weekend day might work well for this purpose.

3. Eat simply. Prepare simple menus that don't require a lot of time to fix. You don't need to eat gourmet meals every-day for your food to be tasty, healthy, and balanced.

4. Pre-wash fruits or vegetables a meal ahead of time so that they will be ready to prepare.

5. Make up all dressings, spreads, gravies, cheese substitutes for the week, then plan your menus around these items. For instance, if I make a double batch of Cashew Gravy I can use it to make Shepherd's Pie, Creamy Zucchini Corn Chowder, or Cabbage Noodle Stroganoff. Depending on how much gravy is needed for each recipe you can probably make all three.

6. Try some of the easy recipes in this book, like; Quick & Easy Black Bean Corn Soup, Fast & Easy Vegetable Stir Fry, Browned Tofu, or Spicy Home Style Potato Fries

WHAT IS TOFOOOO?

"Yuck, what's this white stuff in the spaghetti mom?" Asked eight-year-old Brittany. "It looks like cottage cheese," she added with a frown contorting her face.

"Its tofu and its good for you," Replied her mother Kathy. "Now eat up!"

"What's tofoooo?" Asked Brian her four year old. His little face held a curious expression.

"It's like cheese made from soybeans," said Kathy trying to simplify her answer for Brian to understand.

"I hate beans," said Brittany.

"I hate beans too." Echoed Brian.

"Children," began Kathy with a sigh, "I know that tofu is something new to our table, but a least give it a try. You just might like it, and it doesn't taste like beans." She said trying to convince even herself.

Kathy had purchased tofu for the first time in her life and had no idea what to do with it. But she had been hearing a lot about the great health benefits of tofu so she decided to give it a try. How bad could it be? It was hard enough trying to find the tofu in the grocery store. Was it in a box, a can, was it frozen or refrigerated? When Kathy finally located the tofu in the cooler, she didn't know which texture she should buy, the silken, soft, firm or extra firm. She finally decided on the soft variety.

When Kathy got home, she began her food preparations for dinner. She opened the package of tofu and discovered that it was softer than she had expected. What should she do with it? She had no clue. Kathy sliced a bit off the cake and tasted it. Hmm, she paused pushing the tofu around in her mouth trying to analyze its taste. It had little or no flavor she thought to herself, in fact it was awful. She was tempted to throw it away, but finally decided to crumble it up into some spaghetti sauce, hoping the sauce would disguise it and give it flavor. As she placed the spaghetti dish on the table, she prayed the kids wouldn't notice the tofu in it. But Brittany spotted the white pieces of tofu the minute the spaghetti got on her plate.

"I don't like it mom," whinned Brittany.

"Me neither," said Brian, shaking his little head from side to side for added emphasis.

"Okay kids." Replied Kathy, not wanting to turn dinner into a war zone, "I'll go make you some peanut butter and jelly sandwiches."

Kathy took up their plates and disappeared into the kitchen.

Have you had a bad experience with tofu? Would you like to know more about tofu and how to make it taste edible and even delicious? Keep reading.

THE SCOOP ON TOFU

Tofu is the product of the soybean, and is composed of pressed protein curds that have been separated from soybean milk through coagulation. Tofu is a bland tasting food, which basically functions as a protein base for many recipes ranging from spicy dishes to sweet desserts. Tofu is very versatile and can be used in a variety of ways. Because of its bland taste and porous texture, it can be infused or seasoned to take on practically any flavor. I don't recommend that you eat it plain unless you like it that way. Tofu can be used in stir-fry's, veggie burgers, soups, and casseroles. Tofu makes a nice creamy base for dressings, mayonnaise, sauces, puddings, ice cream, cheesecake, and many other foods.

Tofu is sold in four different textures: silken, soft, firm, and extra firm. The silken and soft textures are good for puddings, dressing, sauces, or scrambled tofu and tofu cheesecake. The firm and extra firm textures are good for slicing, cubing, baking, browning, grilling, or for use in various protein dishes. Tofu comes packaged in water, once opened the water should be drained off. Any leftover tofu should be stored in an air tight container and should be covered with water one half inch over the top of the tofu and kept refrigerated. The water will need to be changed every other day to keep tofu fresh. Tofu can also be frozen to change its texture from a soft cottage cheese-like texture to a chewy spongy texture. The frozen texture of tofu is ideal for dishes where a meatier texture is desired. Because of its sponge-like texture it readily soaks up any flavor you add to it. Once frozen tofu cannot be blended into a creamy state.

HOW IS TOFU MADE?
- First the soybeans are soaked overnight in water, and then drained.
- Next the rehydrated beans are ground together with a little boiling water to make a mash. The mash is then spooned into a pot of boiling water. The boiling process goes on for about ten minutes, which results in a milky substance called soymilk.
- The soymilk is filtered to separate it from the soybean pulp, and then a small amount of Magnesium Chloride (a derivative of sea salt) is added to coagulate the milk into curds. Lemon juice or Nagari seaweed will also coagulate the milk.
- After the milk coagulates, the curds float to the top of the liquid, and are scooped off and put into forming containers with small holes in them for proper drainage. A lid is placed on the container along with a weight to press out the excess liquid and to form the tofu into shape. It takes several hours for this to happen.
- Once the tofu is fully drained and shaped, it is emptied into a tub of cold water and allowed to sit for another hour.
- Now the tofu is ready to be packaged and sold.

WHERE DO YOU PURCHASE TOFU?

There was a time when the only place you could find tofu, was at an Oriental market or a health food store. But now with the growing popularity and information about tofu, you can now find it at your local grocery store. Tofu can be found usually in a cooler somewhere in the produce department or shelved with the cheeses, yogurts and other dairy products.

WHAT ARE THE HEALTH BENEFITS OF TOFU?

- Tofu is very rich in protein. Three ounces of tofu contains approximately 10 grams of protein, this will vary according to the texture of tofu you are using. Extra Firm tofu has the highest content of protein.
- Tofu is high in calcium, which can reduce the risk of osteoporosis.
- Soy products are high in fiber and cholesterol free and can reduce the risk of heart disease.
- Soy products contain isoflavones a naturally occurring plant form of estrogen, which helps reduce the risk of breast cancer and eases the symptoms of menopause.
- Tofu is dairy free and good for those with lactose intolerance.
- Tofu contains the required amount of essential amino acids for tissue repair and growth.
- Certain sugars in the soybean help promote the growth of good bacteria in the colon called bifidobacteria, which helps in lowering the risk of colon cancer.

SUGGESTED TOFU RECIPES IN THIS BOOK (SEE INDEX)

- Browned Tofu
- Tofu Cheesecake
- Tofu Cashew Mayo
- Tofu Potato Scramble
- Tofu Cashew Sour Cream
- Spicy Sunshine Tofu Dressing or Dip

VEGGIE BLUES

"Eat those peas!" Stacy yelled at her five year old son Timothy for the tenth time that evening. Startled by her tone Timothy picked up his spoon and sullenly began to scoop cold peas into his mouth. Stacy sighed as she turned her attention back to dishwashing, she hated yelling and guilt stung her conscience, but what else could she do? Timothy simply wouldn't cooperate. He had managed to turn dinner into a one hour "eat your peas project." He was such a picky eater, especially when it came to eating his vegetables.

As of late, Stacy had been devoting a lot of time to reading books on the healthy benefits of eating more fruits and vegetables. As a single mom she wanted the best for herself and for her growing son and thus had decided to improve their diet by including more fresh fruits and vegetables. Timothy loved fruit, but strongly disliked anything green like broccoli, spinach, string beans, asparagus and the dreaded peas. Anytime Stacy served a green vegetable Timothy would pout, protest, and then take forever to eat it.

Five minutes later Stacy turned to find her son amusing himself by sliding peas one by one onto his fork while softly humming to himself. Frustrated, Stacy grabbed his fork, snatched up his plate, and without a word scraped the peas into the trash can. Timothy grinned victoriously, slid out of his chair and raced off to play.

Stacy has a big problem. She wants her son to eat vegetables, but he will not eat them. She is becoming extremely frustrated, what can she do?

SUGGESTIONS

It is a rare child who naturally relishes vegetables, unless they've been raised on the stuff and their taste buds haven't been perverted by junk foods. So is it impossible to get children to eat their veggies? Hardly, though initially it will take a lot of firm patient consistency on your part. Below are some suggestions on how to make the transition to eating more vegetables easier and more enjoyable for you and your child.

- Educating your child about the helpful benefits of fruits and vegetables can be helpful for some children. Going beyond just saying "It's good for you," might grab their attention. Explain the nutritional qualities contained within each fruit or vegetable, and don't wait until meal time to do this. Let education begin before you get to the dinner table.

- Serve vegetables first before any other food. Your child is more likely to relish what is first served when he is most hungry.

- Serve vegetables of different colors together to enhance their appeal. Kids are attracted to color. Color is used all the time to attract the attention of children, from colorful clothes and toys, to candy and cereal. Use color to attract your child's interest to their vegetables, and even if they still don't like the vegetable, they may be more incline to at least try them.

- Season vegetables or serve them with your child's favorite sauce or dressing.

- If there is a particular vegetable your child doesn't like, don't serve it alone. Mix it with another vegetable that your child does like, the combination may be more pleasing.

- Be firm yet loving. If your children knows that they can get away with not eating their vegetables they will persist on having their own way until they break you and you cave in to their wishes. Remember that you are the parent, not the child.

- Garnish vegetables before serving them. Purchase some mini garnishing cutters and use them to cut flower, heart or star shapes from slices of hard vegetables like carrots, beets, parsnips, or cucumber (garnishing cutters look like mini cookie cutters). This will take a little time but it might be well worth the effort. Let the children help; they love to eat what they help to prepare.

• Try some of the recipes in this book and see if your child likes any of them. I would suggest the Crispy Breaded Plantain, Cheesy Cauliflower Casserole, or the Glazed Baby Carrots.

MORNING RUSH

It was 8:45 a.m. Mr. Robert Banks was late for work and in a hurry; he had exactly five minutes to get out the door and into his car, then a ten-minute ride to be at his office by 9:00 am. He took a quick glance in the mirror, ran a comb through his hair and adjusted his tie. He quickly grabbed his briefcase and overcoat and headed downstairs. He breezed past his wife Shirley and two children, Jake and Cassy who were seated at the kitchen table eating breakfast.

"Aren't you going to eat breakfast Robert," His wife asked imploringly.

"No, I'm late for work and I gotta go." He replied impatiently.

"But this is the third time this week you've left for work without eating," She stated, concern etching her delicate features.

"I know," he said apologetically, "As soon as things slow down at the office, I promise I'll get back on schedule."

Robert kissed his wife on the forehead, ruffled his son's curly mop of hair and gave his daughter a quick hug, and was out the door. The car roared to life as he raced out of the driveway.

Robert was a successful lawyer who started a law firm with his good friend from college, Daniel Brockman. Together they opened their own law office called the Brockman & Banks Law Firm. With so many court dates, business meetings, luncheons, and new clients to meet, he never seemed to find time to slow down and take care of himself. He was always on the go.

Impatiently waiting at a stoplight, he decided to pull over to the Donut Shop drive-thru to get a quick cup of coffee and a donut. After all he was hungry. Hopefully the donut would stall his hunger until lunch.

With briefcase and donut in one hand and coffee in the other, Robert walked into his office already brewing with activity to begin the day.

Do you have mornings like this? Do you skip breakfast? What can you do to solve your dilemma?

SUGGESTIONS:

Breakfast; which actually means to Break-fast is the most important meal of the day. After waking from a night of fasting, it is important to eat a hearty breakfast to fuel us up for the day's activity. Running out of the house without breakfast is like taking your car on a long trip without any gas in the tank. Without fuel food in your tank, your body cannot function at its optimal peak. A cup of coffee, a donut, or a quick bowl of cereal is neither adequate nor healthy food choices for breakfast. You need a balanced meal with plenty of fresh fruits, complex carbohydrates (fuel and energy), vegetable protein (body builders), plus in general, the meal should be low fat, high in fiber and prepared with natural ingredients.

When you start the day off right, you can expect to feel good, and function at your best. So eat a good breakfast!

Below are some tips to get you started in the right direction:

1. Make eating breakfast a priority. Love yourself enough to give your body what it needs.
2. Get up earlier so that you will have more time to include breakfast. Buy an alarm clock if necessary.
3. Prepare breakfast foods the night before. You will find it much easier when breakfast foods are already made, this will conserve time and energy.
4. Make a weekly breakfast menu, so you're not stressing yourself out trying to think of what to make every morning.
5. Try some of the great recipes in this book, like; Special Breakfast Oatmeal, Fruited Couscous, or the Breakfast Berry Crunch. Yummy!

I DON'T KNOW HOW TO COOK!

"What am I doing?" Screamed Karen in sheer frustration. "I can't even boil a pot of water, what am I even doing in this kitchen!" Her eyes surveyed the mess around her. A pot of cooking pasta had boiled over on the stove; there were empty boxes and cans littering the counter. There was flour on the floor, on her clothes and even smeared on her face from an earlier accident with a five pound bag of flour. She had tried blending up some hot soup and it had catapulted from the blender like an exploding volcano, spattering her once clean kitchen from ceiling to floor in soup! Karen stood in the middle of the chaos and just cried. She was no cook that was for certain, and all hope of becoming one was slowly turning into despair.

Earlier that day, Karen was so excited about the prospect of trying to seriously cook for the first time. One of her new year's resolutions had been to learn how to cook. So she purposed to teach herself the art. How hard could it be? As a child Karen's mother never allowed her in the kitchen, and as a result she lacked basic food preparation skills. So far she had gotten by on fast food, restaurant fare and frozen food dinners which she would warm up in her microwave oven, but eating like this was taking its toll on her health. She had to do better and today was the day! She had carefully assembled all her ingredients and pulled out a few cook books which she had recently purchased. She also took out her pots, mixing bowls, and utensils and began her cooking adventure fully confident that all would go well, but alas, nothing turned out like she had planned and now here she was crying about it. She stood up and dusted off her clothes, grabbed a broom and began the task of cleaning up.

Okay, maybe you're not as bad off as Karen, but perhaps you share a similar fate? What should you do? Where do you start? Let's talk about it.

SUGGESTIONS:

We are living in a time when cooking is fast becoming a lost art. Cooking has become more of a career choice or hobby, or something that is done only during the holidays. Cooking somehow doesn't quite fit into our fast paced modern lifestyle. Many like Karen are surviving on junk foods that are designed to satisfy hunger but are not necessarily made to meet the nutritional needs of the body.

Cooking is an art that requires knowledge, skill, coordination and a lot of patience. Until you can wear the title of "master chef," here are some tips to help you get there.

1. Search for a cooking class that teaches healthy food preparation in your area that you can attend. Many schools, health food stores and churches offer such classes.
2. If you know someone who knows how to cook, ask them to teach you.
3. Begin educating yourself by reading cook books and informational books about food.
4. Cooking videos are also very helpful.
5. Master a recipe a week until you have enough recipes that you can make well at any given time.
6. Cooking requires skill so don't give up if you don't succeed at every attempt. Keep trying.

I CAN'T AFFORD TO EAT VEGETARIAN.
IT'S TOO EXPENSIVE!

"I can't believe I spent over $175.00 in there!" Martha had just exited her local health food store and was standing in the parking lot staring at her grocery receipt in disbelief. She had three small bags in her hand and couldn't imagine why her bill was so high, and she still had to stop at the grocery store!

Martha had a family of three: herself, her husband Dan, and her eight-year-old son Jeremy. Since becoming a vegetarian, it seemed she spent so much money on food which fueled constant arguments between her and Dan. Dan couldn't understand why eating healthy had to cost so much money, and Martha would argue back that healthy foods cost more than junk foods and that she needed everything on her grocery list in order to make the various foods they ate everyday. But neither of them ever came close to an understanding or a solution. What can Martha do? Do you have this problem too? Check out the suggestions below.

SUGGESTIONS:

Eating vegetarian can be expensive, but it doesn't have to be. There are ways to cut down on food expenses. For instance, you may purchase a pack of frozen veggie burgers (4 in a pack) at your local health food store for almost $4.00 a box and it will only feed a family of 4 for one meal, but you can buy a pound of tofu for under $3.00 and make a batch of burgers at home from scratch and you will spend less money per burger, plus you will end up with almost six burgers!

Buying lots of quick boxed, canned, or frozen prepared foods, especially meat substitutes will be very expensive. Here's a good rule to follow. Buy what you must, but make what you can. Also remember, the more processed the food, the more expensive it is. Eating vegetarian can be affordable; it just takes time and planning.

1. Buy in bulk. Items like flour, oats, rice, dried fruits, nuts, seeds, etc. are much cheaper purchased in bulk rather than buying brand name packaged foods.
2. Avoid or reduce buying useless items like snack foods and treats.
3. Sprout. Sprouting is an easy and inexpensive way to get fresh, organic, nutritious produce right on your own kitchen counter.
4. If you have the time and yard space, grow a garden. Growing your own vegetables and herbs is inexpensive and is a rewarding experience.
5. Don't waste food! Use up leftovers.
6. Find a local health food co-op where you can buy foods by the case and save money.
7. Find a local wholesale produce market that will sell you produce at a reduced rate. Some wholesale markets will allow off the street customers to come in and buy just what you need at the wholesale price.
8. Avoid buying processed or packaged meat substitutes because they are costly and are not the healthiest for your body. Make what you can from scratch.
9. Eat simply. Don't try to make extravagant gourmet meals everyday. The more simple the food, the healthier it is. But avoid the extreme of eating so simply that the food lacks appeal, taste, and nourishment.
10. Make your own bread. Buying whole grain bread at a health food store can be very expensive; especially if you have children in school who need packed lunches everyday with sandwiches in them. Bread will tend to vanish quickly.
11. Make a weekly menu, that way you get exactly what you need for the week eliminating guesswork, and overbuying.

GOT A SWEET TOOTH?

Jason pulled his car into a parking space at the local supermarket. His wife Faye had asked if he could pick up a few groceries on his way home from work. As he walked through the store entrance, a draft heavily saturated with the sweet scent of cinnamon buns wafted across his nose from the nearby bakery. Oh how he loved cinnamon buns! As he turned the corner he could see the clear enclosed bakery shelves lined with the sticky dessert. Next to them were the plump glazed jelly donuts and then the crumb coffee cake. There were cupcakes piled with thick colorful frosting, moist chocolate brownies, and warm chewy oatmeal cookies. The temptation was more than he could bear.

At the age of thirty nine, Jason had been addicted to sweets ever since his long ago college days when he would spend late nights pouring over books with a cup of coffee to keep awake and some delectable sweet of choice. He had tried so many times to cure his "sweet tooth," even substituting fruit for the forbidden pastry, but nothing seemed to work or motivate him to stop his out of control sugar consumption, not even the extra pounds he had managed to pack onto his once lean frame.

Jason now stood transfixed, starring at the array of sweets that seemed to be calling him by name. Unable to resist the temptation any longer, he walked over to the pastry shelf, grabbed a bag and helped himself to three cinnamon buns, two jelly donuts and two jumbo oatmeal cookies. Guilt stung his conscience, but there was no turning back, he already had the coveted treats in his possession and his taste buds were restlessly craving the first bite.

Back in the car, Jason took out his cinnamon buns and began to enjoy bite after bite after gratifying bite, as sugar dumped into his bloodstream at an alarming rate. Next he devoured the jelly donuts and then the cookies. Now guilt hung over him like a cloud, as his conscience condemned and sentenced him to the prison of disgrace. Jason hated that he had no control over his impulses. What would Faye say when he told her he wasn't hungry for the meal she was preparing for him at this very moment? Jason crumbled up the empty bag and stuffed it deep into his coat pocket to conceal the evidence. He started up the car and shamefully headed for home. At least he had Faye's groceries.

Can you relate to Jason's dilemma? Do you have a "sweet tooth?" Is there anything you can do about it? Keep reading.

SUGGESTIONS:

It is important to pay attention to your body's cravings, because cravings can indicate a need the body has for a specific nutrient that is not being supplied by the diet. You may mistake these cravings for something sweet, spicy, salty or even chalky, when in reality your body may be deficient in some vitamin or mineral.

Suppose for a moment that you are craving something sweet and you decide to go eat a donut to cure the craving. The donut will temporarily stop the craving, but the sugar in the donut will deplete the body of nutrients and as a result will make the craving return, sometimes even stronger than before. In time you may even become a sweet addict, always craving sweets with no permanent relief in sight.

Below are some tips that will help you get to the root cause of your cravings.

• Eat a well balanced diet that includes lots of fresh fruits and vegetables. A dietary supplement may be necessary to help insure adequate nutrition.

• Avoid refined foods like white flour and white sugar, as these foods will deplete the body of nutrition. Eat an abundance of dark leafy greens, ripe fruits in season, legumes, along with whole grain breads and cereals.

• Drink plenty of water to help purify the taste buds.

- Eat meals at regular times each day to avoid grabbing the wrong foods when you are in a hurry to eat.

- Use honey instead of sugar. Honey, unlike sugar does not rob the body of nutrients, but actually contributes nutrition.

- Never shop for food when you are hungry. It is much harder to resist the temptation for sweets or any other improper food when your stomach is crying out for something to eat.

- Try some of the healthy dessert recipes in this book like Tofu Cheesecake, Honey Spice Sticky Buns, or the Peanut Butter Oatmeal Cookies

BREAD MAKING DISASTER

The timer rang loudly, sending Bill flying into the kitchen to check on his bread that was baking in the oven. He could smell the aromas exuding through the air and he could imagine large golden brown loaves of bread, the pride of any baker, waiting to be sliced and buttered. He slowly opened the oven door to take a peek, and then slammed it shut with severe disappointment. Once again his bread had flopped and it resembled heavy flat bricks, rather than the beautiful loaves of bread he had hoped for. This was the third time he had tried making bread that day with no success. The first time the bread had risen, but it had large gaping holes in the center. The second time he had forgotten the salt and the bread had an awful taste. Now once again for the third time he stared forlornly at another flopped attempt at bread making.

Bill had recently attended a bread making class, and was so inspired by the prospect of being able to make his own bread that he couldn't wait to go home and try it out. The demonstrator had made it seem easy enough. He carefully collected all the necessary ingredients and tools, even purchased a brand new dough mixer. But alas, he wasn't able to make the bread he had dreamed of, even after three tries. "What am I doing wrong?" Bill asked himself again and again. "Maybe I'm not cut out to be a bread maker after all." He sighed as he removed the flat loaves from the oven.

Have you experienced Bill's disappointment with bread making? Do you need some help?

SUGGESTIONS:

Bread making is an art that requires time and patience to perfect. So don't give up after the first try, keep trying until you master the art. Personally I am of the opinion that the person who makes the most mistakes, in time becomes the

23

better bread maker, because they not only know what to do, but also what not to do, which gives them a clearer understanding of the process vs. the person who makes bread for the first time and "lucks" out.

When I make bread I like to make sure that I'm in a good mood and have nothing pressing to do that day. My kitchen needs to be clean and all my ingredients need to be set out. I enjoy working with my favorite music playing in the background. Mood and atmosphere are important to successful bread making. However, you may prefer silence.

So my advice for bread-making disasters is to keep on trying. Analyze each mistake and use it as a stepping-stone to better bread making.

Below are some trouble shooting suggestions to help you figure out what you might be doing wrong.

BREAD WON'T RISE

- Old or poor quality yeast.
- Gluten not sufficiently developed by proper kneading.
- Too many nuts, seeds or raisins added to the bread dough and weighing it down.
- Oven too hot.
- Water for activating the yeast too hot or not warm enough.
- Not enough flour added to give the dough structure.
- Drafty cool kitchen.
- Too much honey or sweetener retards the rising ability of the bread.
- Too much fat added.
- Bread dough overworked, breaking down the gluten.
- Bread placed in a cold oven.
- Too much salt will inhibit yeast activity.

BREAD TOO MOIST OR WET INSIDE

- Oven not hot enough.
- Bread not baked long enough.
- Not enough flour added to give dough texture.
- Bread bagged before it has thoroughly cooled.

BREAD HAS A LARGE HOLE IN THE CENTER
- Improper shaping of loaf.

BREAD HAS SMALL HOLES THROUGHOUT
- Gluten flour with low protein content.
- Gluten not sufficiently developed by proper kneading.
- Too many air bubbles in dough. (Air bubbles need to be pressed out before shaping the dough into a loaf.)

BREAD HAS FLOUR POCKETS INSIDE
- Flour not mixed in thoroughly.

BREAD HAS POOR TASTE
- Salt not added or too much salt.
- Bread allowed to sour by being bagged too soon or by being left out in warm temperatures.
- Honey used with a strong aftertaste.

BREAD IS CRUMBLY AND DRY
- Bread dough allowed to rise too long.
- Too much flour added.
- Gluten not properly developed by stirring and kneading.
- Coarse grain flour.

BREAD HAS STRETCH MARKS ON TOP
- Stressed bread dough. (When bread dough is worked too much it becomes tough and elastic causing stretch marks.)
- Rolling dough up too tightly when shaping the loaf.

I DON'T KNOW WHAT TO COOK!

"I have no idea what to cook!" Sighed Amy as she peered into her half empty refrigerator. Amy had just gotten home from work, hunger was driving her insane and all she wanted to do was EAT! To make something from scratch would take too long and she didn't have the patience. She quickly scanned her kitchen cupboards, desperate for anything to munch on. She spotted a box of vegetable crackers and eagerly took them down and began to eat them greedily.

Turning back to the refrigerator, Amy withdrew a small container of half eaten leftover spaghetti. She placed it in the oven and waited impatiently for the timer to ring, declaring her meager meal ready.

Suggestions

Deciding what to make for each meal of the day can be a mentally draining and time consuming task. Proper meal planning can eliminate a lot of frustration and anxiety when it comes to meal preparation. Below are some tips to help you simplify your life in the kitchen.

1. Make a weekly menu and from your menu make a grocery list. Shop for the items you need so that you will have them on hand when you need them.
2. Don't wait until you are "starving" before you start to fix your food. Have scheduled eating times and start preparing your meal 20–30 minutes ahead of time.
3. When cooking beans, rice, pasta, etc., intentionally cook a little extra for another meal.
4. Make simple easy to fix recipes that don't require a lot of time to complete.
5. Swap casseroles with a trusted friend who cooks the same way you do. Talk about and share menus and suggestions.

6. Have a good collection of cook books available that you can scan through for ideas.

7. Prepare casseroles, soups, and other entrée dishes a meal ahead of time. Keep a couple of casseroles in the freezer for days when you don't feel like cooking. Set aside a special day in the week for making foods specifically to store.

COOKING SUGGESTIONS FOR SINGLES

"This recipe serves four people!" Exclaimed John as he scanned through one of his favorite cookbooks. "What am I going to do with all the extra food? I can't eat it all my myself and even if I cut the recipe in half, I'll still have too much food."

John loved to cook, but everytime he made a recipe, he had enough food to feed an army, and he ended up eating the same thing for the rest of the week! It just wasn't worth the time and effort to do all this cooking for just one person. The telephone rang, startling John from his musing. He hastened across the room to answer it.

"Hello," He answered dryly.

"Hey John, its me, Kevin. You wanna go out and get something to eat?"

"Yeah, why not, I was just sitting here trying to figure out what to cook, but I can't bear another week of eating the same casserole over and over again."

"Well, I'd like to help you out, but you eat all that crazy vegetable stuff!" Kevin chuckled heartily.

"Funny," Replied John. "I'll meet you in fifteen minutes, OK?"

"Yeah, see ya."

John hung up the phone, grabbed his jacket and car keys and headed out the door. He didn't like eating out, but today it seemed to be the easiest alternative.

SUGGESTIONS:

Cooking for yourself presents many challenges, but with proper planning and a little self-motivation, it can be done. Don't look at cooking as a tedious, unnecessary task for only one. Remember, whether cooking for yourself, friends, or family, that food preparation is more than just fixing food to satisfy hunger, its about providing nourishment for the body so that it can function properly. Fast food, junk food, or ill prepared food won't do the job. So take heart, you are important, and your body needs you to care enough to cook! Below are some suggestions to help you get started.

1. When making a casserole recipe meant to feed four or more people, divide the recipe up into small single serving size casserole dishes and freeze them. Casseroles can be kept frozen successfully for up to 3 months. Frozen casseroles provide a quick solution to food emergency situations and for days you don't feel like cooking.

2. Don't consider it troublesome to cook for yourself, set a special plate at your table complete with napkin, fork, knife, and spoon to remind you to take time to eat properly.

3. Choose recipes that are simple and easy to make so that you aren't spending hours in the kitchen preparing your meal.

4. Large recipes meant to feed four or more people can be cut in half by measuring out only half of the required ingredients.

5. Try some of the easy recipes in this book. Fast & Easy Vegetable Stir Fry, Crispy Breaded Tofu Sticks, Haystacks, Super Tossed Salad, Quick & Easy Black Bean Soup.

Easy Vegetarian Lasagna, p. 99

Cornmeal Wheat Waffles, p. 40

Basic Plain Cake, p. 123,
with Whipped Coconut-Creme, p. 127

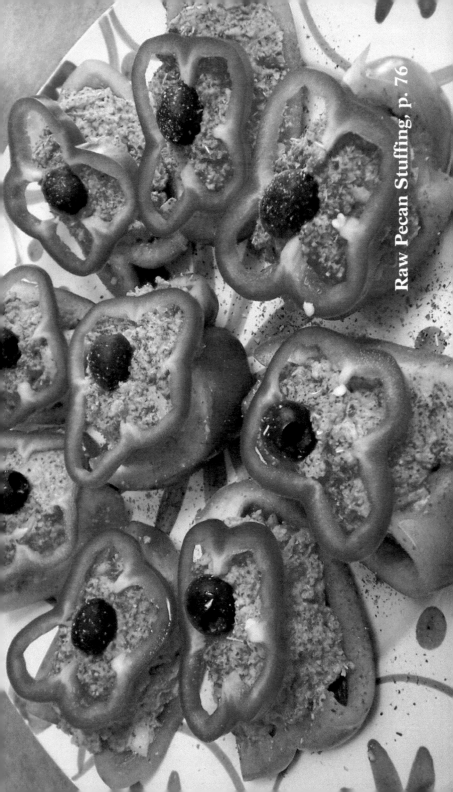

Raw Pecan Stuffing, p. 76

Gluten Pepper Steak, p. 108

Tofu Cheesecake, p. 116

Browned Tofu, p. 96

Tofu eggless salad, p. 66

BREADS

P-Nutty Bread

If you love peanut butter, you're gonna love this bread!

 1½ cups warm water
 ¼ cup honey
 1½ Tablespoons dry active or baking yeast

Dissolve water, honey and yeast in a large mixing bowl, let set until mixture becomes foamy, then add:

 1 teaspoon salt
 1/3 cup smooth peanut butter, natural
 1 cup crushed raw peanuts

Stir mixture until well blended, and then slowly add flours:

 ¾ cup gluten flour
 4 cups whole wheat flour

Beat in flours with an electric hand mixer, dough mixer (KitchenAid®), or a wire whip. When mixture becomes a soft dough, begin kneading with your hands or dough mixer for 5–10 minutes, until dough becomes smooth and elastic. Place dough in an oiled bowl and let rise until double in size, about 10 minutes. Punch down and shape into 2 loaves and place dough into oiled bread pans. Let bread rise again in a warm place for 8–10 minutes, then place in the oven at 350° and bake for 45 minutes or until golden brown. After, remove from bread pans and let set on cooling rack to air-dry. Bag in plastic and store as desired.

Tahini Yeast Biscuits

New and improved easy to follow recipe.

> 1 cup warm water
> 3–4 Tablespoons honey (applesauce or apple
>   juice concentrate may be used)
> 1 Tablespoon dry active yeast

Put water, honey, and yeast into a mixing bowl, stir, then let set for 5–10 minutes until yeast activates. Then add:

> 3–4 Tablespoons tahini (1 tablespoon less
>   makes a lighter dough)
> 1 teaspoon salt

Stir in tahini, and salt, then add:

> 1 cup whole wheat flour

Mix in flour with a wire whip, an electric hand mixer, or a KitchenAid® mixer. Next add:

> ½ cup gluten flour

Mix rapidly with wire whip or if using an electric mixer, turn on high, then slowly add:

> 1 cup whole wheat flour

Mix the last cup of flour in slowly, until mixture becomes a soft dough. Knead briefly for 5–8 minutes. Roll out with a rolling pin about ¼ inch thick and cut with a biscuit cutter. Place biscuits on a greased cookie sheet or use baking parchment paper on the pan. Let biscuits rise in a warm place for 10–15 minutes or until double in size. Place in a preheated oven at 350°. Bake for 25–30 minutes or until lightly brown. Cool on cooling racks

continued

Variation: This recipe can be used to make pizza crust, burger buns, crescent rolls, pizza or fruit filled pockets, danish, etc.

Wonder Lite Cornbread

2½ cups yellow cornmeal
1 cup whole wheat pastry flour
¾ cup gluten flour
1½ teaspoons salt
½ cup honey
½ cup sesame tahini
1½ cups soy milk
1 cup 3% hydrogen peroxide

In a bowl mix together cornmeal, pastry flour, gluten flour, and salt. Drizzle in the honey and tahini, toss well. Pour in together the soy milk and the peroxide. Stir quickly to prevent oxygen loss. Pour batter into a greased pan. Bake at 350° for 30–45 minutes. Let cool before serving.

Quick Peroxide Biscuits

3 cups whole wheat pastry flour
1 teaspoon salt
½ cup sesame tahini

Put the flour, salt, and tahini into a mixing bowl, mix together well, smash any clumps. Add together:

1½ cups soy milk
½ cup 3% hydrogen peroxide

Stir quickly! Use an ice cream scoop to form biscuits. Fill scoop with biscuit mix and place biscuits onto a greased cookie sheet. Bake at 350° for 15–20 minutes or until golden brown.

"Melt in your mouth" Blueberry Muffins

    5 cups whole wheat pastry flour
    1 teaspoon salt
    ½ cup honey
    ½ cup tahini
    1½ cups fresh or frozen blueberries
    1 cup soy milk
    ¾ cup 3% food grade hydrogen peroxide

In a large mixing bowl add flour, salt, honey, tahini, and blueberries. Mix well. Have ready a muffin pan lined with paper muffin liners. Pour in together soy milk and peroxide, stir quickly! Scoop muffin batter into muffin tin molds with and ice cream scoop. Place muffins directly into a preheated oven at 350° for 30–45 minutes or until light brown. Let cool and enjoy!

Onion & Herb Flat Bread

    ½ cup water
    1 Tablespoon tahini
    2 teaspoons salt
    2 Tablespoons onion flakes, dried
    1 teaspoon garlic powder
    ½ teaspoon parsley flakes
    1½ cups whole wheat flour

In a bowl mix together the water, tahini, salt, onion flakes, garlic, and parsley. Slowly add the flour until mixture becomes a soft dough. Cut dough into 6–8 pieces. Roll each piece out into a circle and lightly brown on a hot cast iron skillet for a few minutes on both sides. Flat bread is pliable when hot off the skillet, but will tend to become hard and dry as it sits.

　　Yields approximately 6–8 flat breads.

Crispy Corn Gems

2 cups water

Put water into a small pot and bring to a boil over medium heat, and then stir in with a wire whip:

½ cup onion, chopped
¼ cup sunflower seeds, raw
1 teaspoon onion powder
1 teaspoon garlic powder
1 teaspoon parsley flakes
Salt to taste
¾ cup cornmeal

Stir ingredients together well and cook until mixture becomes very thick, like drop cookie dough batter. Using a spoon, place spoonfuls of mixture onto an oiled cookie sheet, making each gem about the size of a walnut in the shell. Bake at 375° for 30–45 minutes or until lightly brown and crispy.

Serve hot out of the oven with your favorite dipping sauce or dressing.

Yields approximately 15–20 gems.

Mom's Easy Cut–out Biscuits

2 cups whole wheat pastry flour
2 Tablespoons Ener-G Baking Powder
1 teaspoon salt
1 teaspoon Ener-G Egg Replacer
1/3 cup tahini
About ¾ cup soy milk

Mix dry ingredients together thoroughly. Mix in tahini until mixture is crumbly. Add most of the milk and stir to mix. Add more milk as needed to make a soft dough that is soft, but not too sticky. Knead dough gently on a lightly floured

continued

surface 10–12 times. Form into a ball. Pat or roll dough to ½–3/4 inch in thickness. Cut with a biscuit cutter or cut into squares with a knife. Place biscuits on an ungreased baking sheet 1 inch apart. Bake at 450° for 12–15 minutes or until light brown.

Variation: Add ¼ cup of honey for sweet biscuits.

Cornbread

    1 cup whole wheat pastry flour
    1 cup yellow cornmeal
    1 teaspoon salt
    ¼–½ cup honey
    ½ cup tahini
    3 teaspoons Ener-G Baking Powder
    1 heaping Tablespoon Ener-G Egg
       Replacer
    1–2 cups soy milk

Mix all ingredients together in a bowl, except the soy milk. Stir ingredients until well blended, and then add soy milk, stir again. Pour batter into a greased pan. Bake at 350° for 30–35 minutes.

BREAKFAST

Tofu'n Potato Scramble

½ pound firm or soft tofu, mashed
2 medium boiled potatoes, cubed
1 small onion, diced
½ green pepper, diced
1–2 Tablespoons tahini
1 teaspoon salt
1 teaspoon garlic powder
2 teaspoons chives
1/8 teaspoon turmeric
Dash of cayenne pepper

Put all ingredients into a non-stick skillet, and cook over medium heat until lightly browned.

Serving Suggestion: Serve with grapefruit orange salad and toast.

Variation: Use diced fresh zucchini instead of potatoes.

Jamaican Style Oatmeal Porridge

Recipe by: Olive Manns

3 cups water
2 large bay leaves

Put water and Bay leaves into a pot and bring to a boil over medium heat for about 15 minutes. Add:

½ cup soymilk
1 teaspoon pure vanilla extract
1 cup oatmeal

continued

Stir gently and let simmer for 20 minutes. Sweeten to taste, and serve.

Tofu Omelet

> 2/3 cup tofu, extra firm (mash tofu and
>   pack into measuring cup)
> 1 heaping Tablespoon cornstarch
> ½ teaspoon onion powder
> ½ teaspoon garlic powder
> ½ teaspoon salt
> 1/8 teaspoon turmeric powder
> ½ cup boiling water

Put all ingredients into an electric blender and blend until smooth. Pour about ¼ cup of batter onto a hot non-stick skillet and cook over medium heat until almost dry on top. Place filling on one half of omelet and flip the other side over top. Remove from pan and serve on a plate while hot. Makes approximately 3 small omelets or 2 large. You may need to dab your pan with a little olive oil if omelets stick to the pan.

Potato Filling for Omelet

> 2 boiled potatoes, cubed
> 2 Tablespoons tahini
> 1 small onion, diced
> 1 teaspoon onion powder
> 1 teaspoon garlic powder
> 1 teaspoon salt
> ¼ teaspoon paprika
> Dash of cayenne pepper, optional

Put all ingredients into a non-stick skillet and brown over medium heat for approximately 15–20 minutes or until well browned. Vegetables like zucchini, cauliflower, broccoli flowerets, or diced carrot can be added to the omelet.

Special Breakfast Oatmeal

> 3 cups water
> ¼ cup shredded coconut, unsweetened
> ½ cup raisins
> ¼ teaspoon salt

Put all ingredients into a pot, cover with a lid, and bring to a boil over medium heat. Boil for about 15–20 minutes or until the raisins become plump. Replace water if it begins to boil away. Turn heat off and add:

> 1 cup quick oats
> ¼ teaspoon coriander seed, powder

Do not stir, let oats settle and soak up liquid. Keep lid on pot. Once the oats have absorbed all the liquid, stir gently and serve. Oatmeal may be sweetened with a little honey and a splash of soy milk. Serves 1–2 people.

Breakfast Berry Crunch

In a cereal bowl layer:

> 1½ cups fresh strawberries, wash and remove green leaves. Slice in half lengthwise.
> ½ cup fresh blueberries, washed
> 1 single serving size container of soy yogurt, flavor of choice
> Sprinkle the top with ½ cup of your favorite granola

Enjoy!
Yields 2 servings.

Cornmeal Wheat Waffles

> 1 cup yellow cornmeal
> 1–1½ cups whole wheat pastry flour
> 1 teaspoon salt

Put cornmeal, flour, and salt into a mixing bowl. Set aside.

> 1 heaping Tablespoon flaxseed, ground
> 4 Tablespoons water

Put flaxseed and water into a small pot and cook until mixture becomes slimy. Pour flaxseed mixture into a blender and add:

> 4 Tablespoons sesame tahini
> 3 cups soy milk (Edensoy brand preferred)

Whiz flaxseed mixture, tahini, and soy milk in the blender for 3 minutes. Pour into the flour mixture and stir thoroughly with a wire whip. Once stirred, do not stir again. Pour batter onto a hot non-stick waffle iron to bake. Each waffle should take approximately 6–8 minutes to cook, or when the "ready" light on your waffle iron goes off.

Variation: Eliminate the 1 cup of cornmeal and replace with 1 cup of whole wheat pastry flour, totaling 2 cups of whole wheat pastry flour. Add 1 cup of fresh or frozen blueberries to make blueberry waffles. Yields approximately 5 waffles.

Fruit Sauce

Great for waffles or pancakes!

In a pot add:

> 3 cups of fresh or frozen fruit of choice
> ¾ cup sweetener of choice
> 1 teaspoon pure vanilla extract, alcohol free

Bring fruit, sweetener, and vanilla to a simmer over medium heat. While fruit is cooking mix together in a small bowl:

> 1–2 Tablespoons cornstarch
> 2–4 Tablespoons water

Mix cornstarch and water together and pour into the simmering fruit while stirring to prevent lumps. Cook sauce until thickened, and then serve.

Coconut Pancakes

> 1 cup whole wheat pastry flour
> ½ cup shredded coconut, unsweetened
> 1 teaspoon salt
> 2 Tablespoons sesame tahini
> 1 ½ teaspoons Ener-G Baking Powder
> 1 ½ cups soy milk

In a mixing bowl combine together flour, coconut, salt, tahini, and baking powder. Mix well, the add the soy milk. Mix well only once. Make pancakes on a large non-stick skillet.

Yields approximately 6 medium pancakes

Plum Apple Bread Bake

  4 slices whole wheat bread, cubed
  ½ cup canned plums, chopped
  ½ cup pecans, chopped optional
  ½ cup raisins
  2 Tablespoons honey or apple juice concentrate
  1 teaspoon coriander
  2–3 cups applesauce, unsweetened

Combine all ingredients together in a mixing bowl. Stir well. Put mixture into a glass baking dish. Bake at 350° for 30–45 minutes. Serve with sliced banana and soy milk.

Veggie Breakfast Burrito

  4 wheat flour tortillas

Set aside and make filling:

  2 cups gluten strips (*You may use the recipe in this book for gluten called* **"Wheat Meat"**, (**see recipe, p. 110**))
  1 zucchini squash, cubed
  1 small onion, sliced
  ½ green pepper, cut into strips
  1 teaspoon olive oil or 1 Tablespoon sesame tahini
  1 teaspoon Italian seasoning
  Pinch of cayenne pepper

In a non-stick pan combine the above ingredients. Brown over medium heat for a few minutes. Lay tortillas down on a flat surface and spread each one with your favorite sauce or dressing, (*some good recipes in this book are* **Cashew Sunflower Mayo, Creamy Cucumber Dressing, Pimiento Cheese Sauce, Tofu Sour Cream,** *or you can use ketchup or spaghetti sauce*). Spoon filling onto the edge of each tortilla and roll

continued

up. Place on a cookie sheet and bake at 350° for 15–20 minutes or until lightly browned.

Serving Suggestion: Serve burritos with fresh cubed pineapple or your favorite citrus fruit.

Other recipes in this book may be used as filling like: **Vegetarian Chili**, **Tofu n' Potato Scramble**, **Browned Tofu**, and **Browned Eggplant**.

Fruited Couscous

    2 cups couscous, cooked
    2 cups fruit, canned, fresh, or frozen (peaches,
       blueberries, strawberries, pears, etc.)
    ¼ cup raisins
    ½ teaspoon coriander
    1 teaspoon vanilla extract, alcohol free
    ¼ cup honey

Mix all ingredients together in a mixing bowl. Serve with soymilk and a little honey.

Vegetarian Breakfast Sausage Patties

    1¾ cups water
    5 Tablespoons Bragg's Liquid Aminos
    2 teaspoons garlic powder
    3 Tablespoons onion flakes

Put the water, liquid aminos, garlic powder, and onion flakes into a small pot. Bring to a boil over medium heat. Turn heat off mix the following ingredients into a mixing bowl.

    ¾ cup TVP®, granules (texturized vegetable
       protein)
    1 cup boiling water

continued

Pour boiling water over TVP®, let soak until all the water is absorbed, and then add:

> 2 cups rolled oats
> 1 cup walnuts, ground
> 1 ½ teaspoons sage powder
> 1 teaspoon Italian seasoning
> ½ teaspoon thyme
> ¼ teaspoon cayenne pepper
> Salt to taste

Mix the above ingredients with the soaked TVP®. Add bowl contents to the liquid ingredients in the pot. Stir gently and cover pot with a lid. Let mixture set for 20 minutes, or until all the liquid is absorbed. Form into small patties and place on an oiled cookie sheet. Bake at 350° for 20 minutes on one side, turn patties over and bake for another 10–15 minutes or until crispy and brown.

Yields approximately 15 patties.

Peanut Butter & Applesauce Toast

Spread a moderate layer of peanut butter on a piece of toasted bread and top with the desired amount of applesauce. Sliced banana can be placed on top in place of the applesauce.

Apple Biscuit Cobbler

10 lrg. Granny Smith apples, peeled and sliced
½ c. honey
2 tsp. vanilla extract
1 tsp. coriander, ground
½ c. water

Put sliced apples into a pot; add honey, vanilla, coriander, and the water. Cover the pot with a lid and cook apples over low heat until they have shrunk in volume and are slightly tender. In a small bowl mix together,

1 Tbs. cornstarch
3 Tbs. water

Stir together well. Pour cornstarch mixture slowly into the cooking apples while stirring constantly. Cook apples until thickened. Pour into a baking dish and set aside. Make one batch of **Quick Peroxide Biscuits** (see recipe, p. 33). Scoop biscuit batter on top of the apples, place immediately into a preheated oven set at 350°. Bake for 30–45 minutes until golden brown.

SPREADS, DRESSINGS, SAUCES, & GRAVIES

Spicy Sunshine Tofu Dressing or Dip

Makes 1 pint.

> ½ pound tofu, extra firm
> 1 teaspoon pizza seasoning
> ¼ teaspoon turmeric
> ½ teaspoon garlic powder
> 1 teaspoon onion powder
> 2 teaspoons salt
> ¼ teaspoon cayenne pepper
> 3 Tablespoons lemon juice
> ½ cup hot water

Put all ingredients into an electric blender and blend until very smooth, about 5 minutes. Then add while still blending:

> ½ cup cashews (add ¼ more cashews if a thicker sauce is desired)

> Blend until smooth. Pour dressing into a container and refrigerate until set (overnight is best). Dressing will thicken to the consistency of mayonnaise. Once set, stir in if desired:

> ¼ cup drained sweet pickle relish, (use relish of choice), optional

This dressing or dip may be used on salads or as a dip for veggies. It makes a great dip for **Crispy Breaded Tofu Sticks**. (*see recipe, p. 100*)

Sweet Basil Dressing

        1 cup cashews
        ¾ cup sunflower seeds
        1 cup honey
        ¾ cup lemon juice
        8 sprigs fresh basil
        1 Tablespoon salt
        2 cloves fresh garlic, peeled
        1 cup water

Put all ingredients into a blender and blend until smooth. Refrigerate.

Cashew Sunflower Mayo

Recipe by: Danielle Dawson

This mayo is thick and creamy and doesn't separate. It holds up very well in macaroni and potato salad and is the best homemade, egg and oil free mayo I've ever tasted!

        2 cups cashews
        ½ cup sunflower seeds
        1 cup lemon juice
        1 cup honey
        1 medium onion, peeled
        1 Tablespoon salt
        1 cup water

Put all ingredients into a blender; blend for 8–10 minutes or until smooth, (a Vita-Mix® blender works best for this recipe).

Refrigerate to set.

Turkey Style Gravy

This gravy tastes great over mashed potatoes.

>1 cup water
>3–4 Tablespoons Bragg's Liquid Aminos
>½ teaspoon onion powder
>1 teaspoon garlic powder
>½ teaspoon salt

Put all ingredients into a saucepan and bring to a rapid simmer. Mix together in a small measuring cup or bowl:

>1 heaping Tablespoon unbleached white flour
>3 Tablespoons ice cold water

Pour flour water mixture into gravy to thicken, while stirring constantly to prevent lumps. Serve over mashed potatoes, brown rice, etc.

Fat Free Italian Dressing

>1 teaspoon Italian seasoning
>1 teaspoon garlic, granulated
>½ teaspoon onion, granulated
>1 teaspoon salt
>¼ teaspoon Xanthan gum

Put the above ingredients into a pint jar, and add:

>½ cup lemon juice
>½ cup water

Put a screw lid on the jar and shake until dressing is well blended. (***Do not put this dressing in the blender. The blending action will make it slimy.***)

Tangy Creamy Dill Dressing

    1 cup sunflower seeds
    1 teaspoon garlic powder
    1 teaspoon onion powder
    1 teaspoon salt
    2 teaspoons dill weed, dry
    ¾ cup lemon juice
    2 cups water

Put all ingredients into the blender and blend until smooth.

Refrigerate to chill.

Use as desired.

Spicy Green Pepper Ranch Dressing

    1 cup cashews
    1 medium green pepper, remove stem and
        seeds
    ½ cup lemon juice
    1 cup soy milk
    1 teaspoon oregano
    1 teaspoon cumin
    1 teaspoon Italian seasoning
    1 teaspoon garlic powder
    1 teaspoon onion powder
    2 teaspoons salt
    ¼–½ teaspoon cayenne pepper

Put all ingredients into an electric blender and blend until smooth and creamy.

Refrigerate to chill.

Use as desired.

Creamy Ranch Style Dressing

1 cup **Tofu Cashew Sour Crème** (*see recipe,*
    p. 53)
2 teaspoons garlic powder
1 teaspoon oregano
Add soy milk until desired consistency

Mix all ingredients together un a bowl until smooth.

Sweet & Spicy Tahini Dressing

1 cup sesame tahini
¼ cup lemon juice
1/3 cup honey
1 teaspoon garlic powder
1 teaspoon onion powder
2 teaspoons salt
2 teaspoons paprika
Dash cayenne pepper
Soymilk

Put first eight ingredients into a bowl and mix well, and then add soymilk until desired consistency is achieved.

Tangy Oregano Tahini Dressing

1 cup sesame tahini
½ cup lemon juice
1–2 teaspoons oregano, dry
2 Tablespoons onion flakes, dry
2 teaspoons garlic powder
1 teaspoon salt
Soy, rice, or almond milk

In a bowl add tahini, lemon juice, oregano, onion flakes, garlic powder, and salt. Stir, mixture will become extremely thick. Add milk and stir until desired consistency is achieved. This dressing becomes very thick in the refrigerator and may

continued

need to be thinned out with a little more milk. Dressing will last refrigerated for up to 2 weeks.

Creamy Cucumber Dressing

    1 cup sunflower seeds or cashews, raw
    1 large cucumber, peeled
    ½ cup lemon juice
    ½ cup honey
    1 Tablespoon onion powder or 1 small
      onion, peeled
    1–2 teaspoons salt
    1 cup water

Put all ingredients into a blender and blend until smooth and creamy. Refrigerate to chill.

Variation: 2 stalks of celery can be used in place of the cucumber to make creamy celery dressing.

Note: *Because this dressing is raw it will separate once refrigerated, leaving a liquid layer on the bottom of the container. Simply stir and mix together again. You may also notice strong gaseous odors that will disappear once the dressing is stirred.*

Tofu French Dressing

    1 pound tofu, extra-firm
    3 Tablespoons tomato paste
    ½ cup lemon juice
    4 Tablespoons honey
    2 teaspoons salt
    1 teaspoon onion powder
    1–2 teaspoons garlic powder

Put all ingredients into a blender and blend until smooth.

Tofu Cashew Mayo

  1 pound tofu, extra-firm
  ¼–½ cup honey, optional
  2 teaspoons salt
  ½ cup lemon juice
  ¼–½ cup cashews, raw

Blend all ingredients in a blender until smooth.

Refrigerate. Mayonnaise will become thicker once refrigerated.

Tofu Cashew Sour Crème

  ½ pound tofu, extra-firm
  ½ cup lemon juice
  1–2 teaspoons salt
  ½ teaspoon garlic powder
  ½ teaspoon onion powder
  ¼ cup cashews, raw

Put all ingredients into a blender and whiz on high until smooth.

Refrigerate.

Sour cream will become thicker once refrigerated.
Use on biscuits, crackers, baked potatoes, etc.

Sunflower Sour Cream

  1 cup sunflower seeds, raw
  ¾ cup lemon juice
  2 teaspoons salt
  2 teaspoons garlic powder
  1 cup water

continued

Put all ingredients into a blender and blend until smooth and creamy.

Pour into a container and refrigerate. Sunflower sour cream will thicken once refrigerated.

Use as desired.

Pimiento Cheese Sauce

> 1½ cup cashews, raw
> 1 (16 ounce) can pimientos or 1 red pepper
> ½ cup lemon juice
> 2 Tablespoons sesame tahini
> 2 Tablespoons nutritional yeast flakes
> 2 teaspoons salt
> 1 teaspoon onion powder
> 2 teaspoons garlic powder
> 2 cups water

Put all ingredients into a blender and blend until smooth. Refrigerate. Sauce will become thicker in the refrigerator.

Use Pimiento cheese sauce over vegetables, to make macaroni and cheese, on pizza, to make grilled cheese sandwiches, etc. This sauce becomes thicker and creamier when used in a recipe that goes into the oven to bake.

If a thicker sauce is desired, increase the amount of cashews used to 2 cups.

Golden Cashew Sauce

1 c. cashews
½ c. lemon juice
2 Tbs. sesame tahini
1 tsp. turmeric powder
1 Tbs. nutritional yeast flakes
1 tsp. onion powder
1 tsp. garlic powder or 2 cloves of fresh garlic
2 tsp. salt
1½ c. boiling water

Put all ingredients into a blender and blend until smooth.
Add a little more water if needed.

Refrigerate.

Use this sauce over vegetables, pasta, rice, etc.

Tahini Garlic Sauce or Dressing

1 cup sesame tahini
4 Tablespoons honey
3 cloves fresh garlic, minced
1 teaspoon onion powder
1 Tablespoon parsley flakes
1–2 teaspoons salt
Soy milk

Put all ingredients into a small mixing bowl, except the soy
milk (save for last). Stir until mixture is very thick and then
add soy milk, mixing in slowly until desired consistency is
reached.

Refrigerate.

Use this sauce over vegetables or over a tossed salad.

Bekki's Zesty Lemon Tomato Bang

    4 Tablespoons ketchup of choice
    1 cup lemon juice
    2 Tablespoons honey
    1 teaspoon Italian seasoning
    1 teaspoon salt

Put all ingredients into a pint size glass jar and shake until well blended.

Use over salad.

Tomato Basil Gravy

    2 cups tomato juice
    1 teaspoons onion powder
    1–2 Tablespoons honey
    1 Tablespoon vegetable broth powder of choice
    1 Tablespoon basil fresh or dried

Put all ingredients into a small sauce pan and bring to a gentle simmer. To thicken gravy, add to a small bowl:

    2–3 Tablespoons cornstarch
    4–5 Tablespoons water

Mix cornstarch and water together well, and then pour slowly into the pot with the simmering gravy ingredients while stirring briskly. Cook until thickened. Serve.

On Thyme Gravy

2 cups soy milk
1 Tablespoon Bragg's Liquid Aminos
2 teaspoons vegetable broth powder of choice
1 teaspoon onion powder
½ teaspoon garlic powder
1½ teaspoon thyme, dried

Put all ingredients into a small sauce pan and bring to a simmer over medium heat.

To thicken gravy, add to a small bowl:

1–2 Tablespoons cornstarch
4 Tablespoons water

Mix cornstarch and water together, and then pour into the pot with the rest of the ingredients while briskly stirring. Cook until thickened.

Cashew Gravy

1 cup cashews, raw
¼ cup cornstarch
1 teaspoon onion powder
1 teaspoon garlic powder
4 Tablespoons Bragg's Liquid Aminos
2 teaspoons salt
1 Tablespoon vegetable broth powder, optional
4 cups water

Put all ingredients into a blender and blend until smooth.

Pour gravy into a sauce pan or pot and cook to thicken over medium heat while stirring constantly to prevent sticking and burning.

Pinto Bean Spread

> 1 (12 ounce) can pinto beans, drained
> ¼ cup sesame tahini
> 1/3 cup lemon juice
> 1 Tablespoons Bragg's liquid aminos
> 1 teaspoons garlic powder
> 1 teaspoons onion powder
> 1 Tablespoons nutritional yeast flakes
> 1–2 teaspoons salt

Put all ingredients into a food processor and cream together. Put pureed spread into a mixing bowl and add:

> 1 small onion, diced
> ½ green bell pepper, diced

Stir in the onion and pepper.

Refrigerate spread to chill before serving.

Use this spread for sandwiches, on toast, crackers, or as a vegetable dip.

Mock Tuna

> 2 cups TVP® chunks, dry
> 3–4 cups boiling water

Put TVP® in a bowl and cover with the boiling water. Let soak for 10–15 minutes until TVP® is tender enough to be pierced with a fork and until all the water is absorbed. Drain off and squeeze out any excess water in the TVP®. Put TVP® into a food processor and chop it into very fine shreds or bits. Put into a mixing bowl and add:

> 2 stalks celery, diced
> 1 small onion, diced
> 1 teaspoon kelp, granules or powder

continued

Stir well and add:

> 1½–2 cups **Cashew Sunflower Mayo (*See
> recipe, p. 48*)** or **Tofu Cashew Sour Crème
> (*See recipe, p. 53*)**

Mix well.

Serve Mock Tuna on toast, crackers, or on a bed of lettuce.

Tahini Honey Spread

> 1 cup sesame tahini
> 1/3 cup honey

Put tahini and honey into a bowl and mix together well.

Use this spread on bread, muffins, or cornbread. This spread
can also be used as a glaze or frosting for cake.

Variation: 2–3 Tablespoons of carob powder can be added to
make a carob spread or frosting.

SALADS

Dill Potato Salad

    5 large red potatoes

Wash potatoes, and cube with skin left on. Put potatoes into a pot and cover with water. Boil over medium heat on range until potatoes are tender and can be pierced with a fork. Do not let the potatoes cook too long or they will become mushy. Drain off the water and let potatoes cool. Once thoroughly cooled, put potatoes into a large mixing bowl and add,

    ¼ cup fresh dill, chopped fine
    1 small onion, diced
    ½ cup black olives, sliced
    1 stalk celery, diced
    1 carrot, shredded
    ½ red pepper, diced
    ½ cup can corn, optional

Mix vegetables in with the potatoes and toss gently, then add,

    1–2 cup **Cashew Sunflower Mayo** (*see recipe, p. 48*)

Stir in mayonnaise, then refrigerate until ready to serve.

Tabouli

    1 cup bulgur, dry
    2 cups boiling water

Put dry bulgur and boiling water into a jar with a lid that has a rubber seal, (a canning jar will work). Let bulgur set until it swells and all the water has been absorbed. Take bulgur out of the jar and put into a mixing bowl. Add:

    1 stalk celery, diced
    1 small onion, diced
    1 cucumber, peeled and diced
    1 cup black olives, sliced
    1 tomato, cubed
    1 Tablespoon dried parsley flakes
    ½ cup lemon juice
    1 teaspoon onion powder
    1 teaspoon garlic powder
    1 teaspoon salt

Stir together chopped vegetables, lemon juice, and seasonings. Chill.

Serve Tabouli as is or on a bed of lettuce with **Sweet & Spicy Tahini Dressing**, (*see recipe, p. 51*).

Three Bean Pasta Salad

    4 cups cooked pasta of choice
    1 cup red kidney beans, can
    1 cup string beans, cooked, can, or frozen
    ½ cup chickpeas
    1 cup black olives, sliced

Stir together pasta, beans, and olives. Set aside and make the lemon juice vinaigrette. In a small jar add:

continued

½ cup lemon juice
2 Tablespoons honey
1 teaspoon dried oregano
1 teaspoon salt
1 Tablespoons tahini, optional

Shake vinaigrette until well mixed, and then pour over pasta salad and toss.

Serve on a bed of lettuce with tomato wedges on top.

Cold Corn Rice Salad

2 cups cooked brown rice
1 cup canned corn
1 stalk celery, diced
½ red pepper, diced
1 small red onion
1 Tablespoon dried parsley flakes
½ c. black olives, sliced

Mix together rice, and chopped vegetables. Chill.

Serve as is or mix with **Cashew Sunflower Mayo** (*see recipe, p. 48*), or with your favorite dressing.

Variation: Couscous, bulgur, or quinoa may be substituted for rice.

Super Tossed Salad

    3 romaine hearts

Wash and break lettuce into bite size pieces and put into a large salad bowl. Add:

    1 cup cooked cold brown rice or pasta
    ½ recipe **Browned Tofu**, use frozen tofu (*see recipe, p. 96*) Cool tofu before adding to the salad.
    1–2 tomatoes cut into wedges
    1 cucumber, sliced with skin
    1 can black olives, whole
    1 small red onion, sliced
    Dash of dried oregano

Toss salad gently.

Serve with favorite dressing and avocado slices.

Quick Cooked Veggie Pasta Salad

    1 box of cooked pasta of choice
    1 bag of frozen mixed vegetables. (Use a mix that has broccoli, cauliflower, and carrots in it)
    1 small onion and red pepper, lightly sautéed
    1 recipe of **Browned Tofu** (*see recipe, p. 96*)

Cook pasta and put into a casserole dish or serving bowl. Lightly steam frozen vegetables with the onion and pepper, and add to the pasta. Brown the tofu and add.

Lightly toss salad and serve with favorite dressing or gravy.

Orzo Black Bean Salad

2 cups cooked Orzo pasta, wheat
1 15 ounce can black beans
1 cup can corn
¾ cup scallions, chopped
½ cup red onion, diced
½ cup red pepper, diced or ¼ cup pimentos,
    chopped
¼ cup fresh dill weed, chopped (fresh oregano
    or basil may be substituted for the fresh dill)

Toss all ingredients together in a large mixing bowl, transfer
to a serving dish and chill in the refrigerator.

Orzo Black Bean Salad Sauce

1 cup **Cashew Sunflower Mayo** (*see recipe,*
    p. 48)
1 Tablespoon chili powder
1 teaspoon cumin powder
1 pinch turmeric
1/3 cup honey
1–2 Tablespoons soymilk

Stir ingredients together in a small bowl until smooth and
creamy. Chill, and then serve.

Tofu Egg-less Salad

1 pound tofu, firm

Put tofu into a bowl and mash with a fork or masher, and then add,

1 stalk celery, finely diced
½ cup onion, finely diced
½ red pepper, finely diced, optional
½ teaspoon turmeric powder
1/8 teaspoon paprika
1 teaspoon onion powder
½ teaspoon garlic powder
1 teaspoon salt

Mix all ingredients together, and then add:

½ cup **Cashew Sunflower Mayo** (*see recipe, p. 48*)

Stir in the mayonnaise, mix well, refrigerate to chill, and then serve on toast, crackers, or a bed of lettuce.

Bulgur Wheat Salad

2 cups bulgur wheat, cooked
1 stalk celery, diced
1 small onion, diced
½ red pepper, diced
1 cup black olives, sliced

Put all ingredients into a mixing bowl, stir and then add,

1–2 cups **Cucumber Dressing** (*see recipe, p. 52*)
or **Cashew Sunflower Mayo** (*see recipe, p. 48*)
2 teaspoons vegetable broth powder, optional

Mix together well and refrigerate to chill. Serve as desired. This salad also makes a nice sandwich spread.

RAW SALADS

Vegan Caesar Salad

    3 romaine hearts, washed and cut

Put lettuce into a mixing bowl and add:

    1 cup **Tofu Cashew Sour Crème (*see recipe,
       p. 53*)**
    ¼ cup slivered almonds
    2 Tablespoons **Mock Parmesan Cheese Substi-
       tute (*see recipe, p. 132*)**
    1 teaspoon oregano, dried

Toss salad gently until all ingredients are well coated with sour cream, then serve.

Tomato, Garlic, & Parsley Salad

    6 medium tomatoes, diced
    4 cloves fresh garlic, minced
    ½ cup fresh parsley, finely chopped
    1–2 teaspoons salt

Mix all ingredients together in a bowl and serve.

Raw Hot Tomato Salsa

6 tomatoes, diced
¼ cup cilantro, finely chopped
1 small onion, diced
½ green pepper, diced
3 cloves garlic, minced
1 teaspoon crushed red pepper
¼ teaspoon oregano, dried
1/8 teaspoon cayenne pepper, or more if
    desired
1–2 teaspoons salt

Mix all of the ingredients together into a bowl. Serve.

Creamy Cucumber Salad

Wash and peel cucumbers. Slice in half lengthwise and scrape out the seeds. Cut cucumber in ¼ inch thick slices diagonally. Put into a bowl and add:

½ red pepper, diced
¼ cup fresh dill weed, finely chopped
1–2 cups **Creamy Cucumber Dressing (*see
    recipe, p. 52*)**

Mix together well, then serve.

Cauliflower Salad

1 head fresh cauliflower

Wash cauliflower, pull or cut floweret sections apart, and then slice thinly with a knife or a hand slicer. Put cauliflower into a bowl and add:

1 cup lemon juice
2 teaspoons salt
2 teaspoons oregano, dried
4 cloves fresh garlic, minced or 2 teaspoons
    dried granulated garlic
1 tsp. turmeric powder

Mix all ingredients together into a bowl and serve.

Salad will turn a bright yellow as it sets.

Tangy Cucumber Dill Salad

This salad tastes like fresh dill pickles!

3 cucumbers, fresh and crisp

Wash cucumbers, leave the skin on, and slice very thin with a knife or hand slicer. Put cucumbers into a bowl and add:

1 cup lemon juice
2 teaspoons dill weed, dried
1–2 teaspoons salt

Mix together and serve.

Zucchini Salad

This salad resembles a pasta salad!

> 3 medium zucchini squash, shredded
> ½ fresh red pepper, diced
> 1 small onion, diced
> ½ can black olives, sliced
> ½ cup lemon juice
> 1 teaspoon Italian seasoning
> 2 teaspoons salt
> 1 tsp. garlic powder
> 1 tsp. onion powder
> ½ cup honey or desired sweetener

Mix everything together in a bowl, and serve. Salad will shrink in volume as it sits.

Farm Fresh Corn & Pepper Salad

> 6 ears farm fresh corn, picked the same day

Shuck corn (remove outer husk and silk hairs) and with a knife cut corn kernels from the cob and put into a bowl. Add:

> ½ green pepper, diced
> ½ red pepper, diced
> 1 small onion, diced
> ½ cup black olives, sliced

Mix ingredients together in a bowl. Serve salad on a bed of lettuce or sprouts and serve with a favorite dressing of choice.

Cucumber Medley

4 cucumbers, washed, peeled, and cubed
½ red pepper, diced
½ green pepper, diced
½ yellow pepper, diced
1 small red onion, diced
½ cup black olives, sliced
1 large tomato, cubed
1 cup lemon juice
1 teaspoon garlic powder
1 teaspoon onion powder
1 teaspoon Italian seasoning
2 teaspoons salt
½ cup honey, optional

Mix all ingredients together in a bowl. Serve.

Shredded Cabbage Salad

½ head red cabbage, shredded or thinly sliced
    on a hand slicer
½ head green cabbage, shredded or thinly
    sliced on a hand slicer
1 carrot, shredded
1 small onion, diced
1 Tablespoon poppy seeds
2 cups **Creamy Cucumber Dressing (*see recipe,
    p. 52*)** or **Fat Free Italian Dressing (*see
    recipe, p. 49*)**

Toss salad together until all ingredients are well coated with
the dressing. Serve. Salad will shrink in volume as it sits.

Green Apple Salad

>   3 hard green apples, thinly sliced
>   ½ cup raisins
>   ½ cup dried unsweetened shredded coconut
>   ¼ cup almonds, slivered, optional
>   2 cups unsweetened pineapple juice

Mix all ingredients together in a bowl, chill and then serve.

Carrot Tuna

>   2 cups carrot pulp from a juice extractor
>   1 stalk celery, diced
>   1 small onion, diced
>   1 teaspoon kelp powder
>   ½ teaspoon salt
>   Add **Creamy Cucumber Dressing** to consistency
>   (*see recipe, p. 52*)

Mix all ingredients together thoroughly. Serve on toast, crackers, or a bed of lettuce.

Grapefruit Lemon Dream Crème Pie

This recipe was inspired by an actual dream I had.

>   ½ cup cold water
>   1 heaping Tbs. Agar powder
>   1 cup boiling water

Whiz the above ingredients in an electric blender for 2–3 minutes. Turn blender off and add:

continued

1½ cup cashews, raw
1 large grapefruit, sectioned and squeezed out
    (2 oranges, whole and peeled, can be used
    instead of the grapefruit if desired)
2 lemons, squeezed
2 teaspoons lecithin granules or liquid
2/3 cup honey or sweetener of choice
½ teaspoon salt
1 teaspoon pure vanilla extract, alcohol free

Turn blender back on and whiz for another 5–8 minutes, or until custardy smooth. Pour mixture into nut pie crust. Chill in the refrigerator to set. Fresh strawberries or sliced banana may be layered under the cream filling. Dress the top of pie with more fresh fruit and a sprinkle of coconut.

Nut Pie Crust

½ cup walnuts, raw and finely ground
1½ cups sunflower seeds, raw and ground to a
    powder
½ teaspoon salt
1–2 Tablespoons water

Mix walnuts, sunflower seeds, and salt into a mixing bowl. Add water one tablespoon at a time until mixture has the consistency of a soft cookie dough. Do not over stir or handle the dough too much or it will become oily and crumbly. Press mixture into a pie pan, and then use.

Cucumber Tomato Dill Salad

    3 cucumbers, sliced thinly with skin on
    2 tomatoes, cubed
    ¼ cup fresh dill weed, chopped fine
    1 cup lemon juice
    1–2 teaspoons salt
    ½ cup honey or sweetener of choice

Put all ingredients into a bowl and toss together well, and then serve.

Raw Pecan Stuffing or Spread

    2 cups pecans, ground fine (Do not substitute
        with pecan meal)
    1 small onion, chopped
    ½ green pepper, chopped
    ½ teaspoon salt
    1 teaspoon onion powder
    1 teaspoon garlic powder
    ½ teaspoon thyme
    ½ teaspoon cumin
    1 teaspoon Italian seasoning
    1 teaspoon Seitenbacher Vegetable Broth Mix

Combine all ingredients together in a mixing bowl, and mix well. Eat alone or use to stuff other vegetables with.

Variation: Add 1 cup of **Creamy Cucumber Dressing** (*see recipe, p. 52*), to make this recipe into a spread for toast, crackers, etc.

Raw Zucchini Spaghetti

3 fresh zucchini

Use a spiral slicer to slice zucchini into thin spaghetti like strands, put into a bowl, set aside, and in another mixing bowl add:

3 tomatoes, diced
6 leaves of fresh basil, chopped
2 cloves fresh garlic, chopped fine
½ teaspoon oregano
1 teaspoon onion powder
1–2 teaspoons salt
2 Tablespoons honey, optional

Mix all ingredients together well. Toss tomato sauce with the zucchini. Serve with **Mock Parmesan Cheese Substitute (*see recipe, p. 132*)**.

Suggestion: Mix zucchini with 1–2 cups of your favorite dressing instead of the tomato sauce.

Fruit or Vegetable Kabobs

Slide the following fruit or vegetable combinations alternately onto kabob sticks.

1st Veggie Combo:

Cherry tomatoes, wash and leave whole
Olives, jumbo whole
Onion, chopped into sizeable chunks
Green pepper, cut into square pieces

2nd Veggie Combo:

Olives, jumbo whole
Cauliflower, pull flowerets into small pieces

continued

Red pepper, cut into square pieces
Broccoli, cut flowerets apart, make small
enough to slide onto stick, but not too small

1st Fruit Combo:

Red grapes, pull grapes from stem
Cantaloupe, cubed
Kiwi, cubed
Strawberries, whole

2nd Fruit Combo

Watermelon, cubed
Cantaloupe, cubed
Honeydew melon. cubed

Serve kabobs with your favorite dressing or fruit sauce.

Orange Date Sauce

2 cups dates, dried

Cook dates in a small pot with water until tender, put into a blender and add:

1 cup orange juice concentrate

Put dates and orange juice into a blender and blend until smooth. Use this sauce for a fruit dip.

Dee's Spicy Raw Onions

    2 large onions, sliced into rings

Put onions into a mixing bowl and add:

    1 teaspoon oregano
    2–3 teaspoons chili powder
    1 teaspoon cumin
    1 teaspoon paprika

Toss onions in the seasonings until thoroughly coated. Onions will shrink in volume as they sit and will look like they've been cooked. Serve with salad.

Lemony Fennel Parsley Salad

    1 fresh fennel bulb

Prepare fennel by cutting off the stalk and the green feathery leaves just above the bulb and remove the bulb outer layer. Split the bulb in half lengthwise from top to bottom and cut off the bulb end. Wash fennel in cold water. Slice fennel thinly using a hand slicer or a knife and put into a bowl. Add:

    Juice from 1 fresh lemon
    ¼ cup fresh parsley, chopped fine
    1 teaspoon salt

Toss together and serve!

Rainbow Pepper Squash Salad

    1 red pepper, diced
    1 orange pepper, diced
    1 green pepper, diced
    2 yellow squash, sliced in circles about ½
        inches thick.
    1 cup black olives, whole

Put cut peppers, squash, and olives into a bowl and add:

    1 teaspoon Italian seasoning
    1 whole lemon, squeezed
    2 Tablespoons honey
    1–2 teaspoons salt

Mix together and serve!

VEGETABLES

Spicy Home style Potato Fries

5 medium white baking potatoes
4 Tablespoons tahini
2 teaspoons paprika
1 teaspoon salt
1 teaspoon garlic powder
1 teaspoon onion powder
Dash of cayenne pepper

Scrub potatoes (leave the skin on), and slice into home-style fries. In a mixing bowl, toss together, potatoes, tahini, paprika, salt, garlic, and onion powder, and cayenne pepper until potatoes are well coated. Spread potatoes onto a cookie sheet evenly. Place into the oven at 400°. Bake for 30–45 minutes or until browned and crispy. Turn over half way through baking time. Serve hot from the oven.

Mashed Potatoes

4 medium Russet potatoes
1–1/2 cup soymilk
1 teaspoon garlic powder
1 teaspoon onion powder
1–2 teaspoons salt

Peel and cook potatoes until very tender. Put into a bowl and mash with a masher.

Add soymilk, garlic and onion powder and salt and gently stir in. Don't stir too much or potatoes will become too stiff. Mashed potatoes can be kept warm in the oven.

Browned Eggplant

1 large eggplant, peeled and cut into cubes
3 Tablespoons tahini
1 teaspoon garlic powder
1 teaspoon onion powder
2 teaspoons Italian seasoning
1 teaspoon salt
1 teaspoon paprika, optional

Put cubed eggplant into a non-stick pan; add tahini, garlic and onion powder, Italian seasoning, salt, and paprika. Toss, and brown on range over medium heat for about 15 minutes or until well browned.

Serve as is or put into a casserole dish, cover with sauce and pimiento cheese and bake in the oven for 15–20 minutes.

Spicy Cabbage

1 head green cabbage

Cut cabbage into fine strips, put into a large pot and add:

1 green pepper, cut into thin strips
1 medium onion, cut into long pieces
1 teaspoon salt, sprinkle over cabbage
1 teaspoon onion powder
1 teaspoon garlic powder
1 Tablespoon Seitenbacher Vegetable Broth Mix

Cook cabbage on range over medium heat until it cooks down by half, about 15 minutes. Then stir in:

2 Tablespoons tahini

Variation: 1 diced tomato can be added. A dash of cayenne pepper will liven up this dish.

Potato Waffles

    4 medium red potatoes, shredded
    2 Tablespoons tahini
    garlic & onion powder to taste
    1 small onion, finely diced
    1 teaspoon salt

In a mixing bowl add and mix together, potatoes, tahini, garlic and onion powder, onion, and salt. Spread mixture onto a hot non-stick waffle iron and bake until browned and crispy.

Serve with **Cauliflower and Carrot Sauce**, (*recipe follows*).

Cauliflower and Carrot Sauce

    2 cups cauliflower, cut into tiny pieces
    1 cup carrots, thinly sliced

Steam cauliflower and carrots in a pot with a little water until tender, and then add:

    1 cup water
    1–2 Tablespoons Bragg's Liquid Aminos
    1 teaspoon salt
    1 Tablespoon honey
    1 teaspoon parsley flakes

Bring to a simmer. In a small bowl mix together:

    1 Tablespoon cornstarch
    2 Tablespoons water

Pour cornstarch and water mixture into the pot slowly while gently stirring to prevent lumps. Cook sauce until thickened, then serve hot over potato waffles.

Zucchini Corn Scallop

3 fresh zucchini squash, sliced
1 small onion cut in strips
1 green pepper, cut in strips
2 Tablespoons tahini
1 teaspoon onion powder
1 teaspoon garlic powder
1 teaspoon salt
2 teaspoons Italian seasoning

Cut up zucchini, onion, and pepper and put into a non-stick pan. Add tahini, onion and garlic powder, salt and Italian seasoning. Lightly toss and brown over medium heat, until zucchini is slightly tender, but not mushy. Then add to the pan:

3 cups canned diced tomatoes
1 cup sweet corn, fresh, can or frozen

Stir in tomatoes, and corn. Add a dash of salt if necessary.

Serve Zucchini Corn Scallop by itself with garlic bread, or serve over rice or noodles.

Cooked Winter Squash

Use butternut, acorn, or delcotta squash for this recipe.

1 squash of choice, peeled and cut into cubes

Cook squash in a pot and cover with water (water should cover the squash about halfway.) Cook squash until tender and you can pierce it through with a fork, mash squash with a fork or masher, then add,

¼ teaspoon nutmeg, ground
½ teaspoon coriander seed, ground
1 teaspoon vanilla extract, optional
Honey to taste

continued

Stir in nutmeg, coriander, vanilla, and honey, and then serve.

Cooked Summer Squash

Use zucchini, yellow, or patty pan squash for this recipe.

> 4 squash of choice, washed and sliced or cubed
> 2 teaspoons salt

Put squash and salt into a pot and cover with water (about halfway). Bring to a boil over medium heat uncovered. Turn off heat, put a lid on the pot and let set for 5 minutes. Check squash by piercing it with a fork. It should be slightly soft but not mushy or waterlogged. If squash is done, drain off the water, and serve.

You may sprinkle dried basil or Italian seasoning over cooked squash if desired.

String bean Augratin

> 1 pound fresh string beans

Wash beans and pluck off the ends. Put into a glass casserole dish and cover with **Cashew Gravy,** (*see recipe, p. 57*). Make sure the beans are thoroughly covered with the gravy. Put bread crumbs on top and put into the oven uncovered at 350°. Bake until beans are tender and can be pierced with a fork.

Oven Roasted Red Potatoes

> 6 medium red potatoes, cubed
> 2 Tablespoons olive oil
> 1 teaspoon garlic powder
> 1 teaspoon onion powder
> ¼ teaspoon thyme
> 1 teaspoon paprika
> 1 teaspoon parsley flakes
> 1–2 teaspoons salt
> Pinch cayenne pepper, optional

Combine all ingredients into a bowl and toss until potatoes are well coated with seasonings. Put potatoes onto a cookie sheet and cover with foil. Bake at 350° for about 25–30 minutes or until the potatoes are soft enough to be pierced with a fork. Remove foil, toss the potatoes gently and place back in the oven at 400° to brown for about 15–20 minutes.
Serve while hot.

Cheesy Cauliflower Casserole

> 1 large head cauliflower
> 1 medium onion, sliced
> 1 medium red pepper, sliced

Wash cauliflower and cut or pull flowerets apart. Put into a mixing bowl and add onion. Set aside and make:

> 1 recipe of **Pimiento Cheese Sauce (*see recipe,*
> *p. 54*)**
> Bread crumbs

Pour cheese sauce over cauliflower and stir. Put into a glass baking dish and sprinkle the top with bread crumbs. Put into the oven covered and bake at 350° for 25–30 minutes or until cauliflower is soft enough to be pierced with a fork, but not too soft or soggy. Remove cover and continue to bake for another 6–8 minutes to crisp the top.

Crispy Breaded Plantain

> 1 ripe plantain, sliced lengthwise
> Bread crumbs, fine

Cover sliced plantain in bread crumbs, place on a dry cookie sheet. Bake at 350° on one side for 5–8 minutes. Turn over and bake for an additional 5 minutes or until crispy and golden. Serve hot from the oven with your favorite dip or dressing.

Glazed Baby Carrots

> 1 bag frozen baby carrots

Put frozen carrots into a casserole dish and cover with foil. Place in the oven at 350° and bake until carrots have thawed, remove foil put carrots back into the oven and bake until all the water has evaporated from them, and then add:

> 1 Tablespoon parsley, dried
> 2 Tablespoons honey
> 1 teaspoon Earth Balance® Natural Buttery
> Spread, optional

Toss carrots, bake for 5 minutes longer and serve.

SOUPS

Quick & Easy Black Bean Corn Soup

 2 cups black beans, cooked
 1 cup corn, can or frozen
 1 stalk celery, sliced
 1 small onion, diced
 1–2 Tablespoons Bragg's Liquid Aminos
 1 teaspoon salt
 ½ cup water
 Dash of cayenne pepper, opt.

Put all ingredients into a pot and simmer over medium heat until the onion and the celery become tender, then serve.

Creamy Zucchini Corn Chowder

Make one recipe of **Cashew Gravy** (*see recipe, p. 57*).

Pour gravy into a pot and add:

 3 fresh zucchini, cut into cubes
 2 cups corn, can or frozen
 1 small onion, diced
 1 Tablespoon parsley flakes

Cook soup over medium heat until zucchini is tender, but not mushy. Stir soup frequently to prevent burning or scorching.

Serve.

Lentil Couscous Soup

    1 cup dry red lentils
    1 carrot, diced small
    1 small onion, diced
    4 cups water

Put lentils, carrot, onion, and water into a pot and gently simmer over medium heat until lentils reach desired tenderness. (About 20–30 minutes) Add more water if necessary. Next, stir in:

    ½ cup couscous, dry
    1 Tablespoon parsley flakes
    2–3 Tablespoons Bragg's Liquid Aminos
    1 teaspoon salt
    ¼ teaspoon turmeric
    ½ teaspoon onion powder
    ½ teaspoon garlic powder
    Dash of cayenne pepper if desired

Continue to cook soup until couscous puffs up and becomes soft. Add more water if soup becomes too thick. Serve.

Easy Cream of Potato Soup

    5 large potatoes, cubed
    Water

Put potatoes in a pot and cover them with water. Cook over medium heat until potatoes become tender. Drain off cooking water and add:

    1 recipe of **Cashew Gravy** (*see recipe, p. 57*)
    1 small onion, diced
    1 Tablespoon parsley flakes

continued

Continue to cook soup until onions become tender, about 15–20 minutes. Serve.

Suggestion: Corn, broccoli, or cut asparagus can be added instead of potatoes or with the potatoes.

Tomato Noodle Vegetable Soup

> 4 cups water
> 3 Tablespoons tomato paste
> 2 teaspoons Seitenbacher Vegetable Broth Mix
> 1 teaspoon onion powder
> 1 teaspoon garlic powder
> 1 teaspoon salt
> 2 Tablespoons Bragg's Liquid Aminos
> 2–3 Tablespoons honey

Put all ingredients into a pot and bring contents to a gentle simmer over medium heat, then add:

> 2 cups cooked noodles, elbows, shells, or spirals
> ½ pound tofu cubed
> 1 bag of frozen mixed vegetables (A frozen mix of string beans, carrots, and corn.)
> 1 small onion, diced

Cook soup for 15–20 minutes longer, then serve.

Mom's Split Pea Soup

  2 cups dry split peas, sorted and washed
  2 leaks, washed and diced
  2 onions, diced
  2 stalks celery, diced
  ¼ teaspoon thyme
  1 bay leaf
  ¾ teaspoon parsley flakes, dry
  4 cups water

Put all ingredients into a pressure cooker and pressurize for 10 minutes, and then add:

  Pinch of cayenne pepper
  Salt to taste

Stir and serve.

Mock Chicken n' Rice Soup

In a pot add:

  4 cups water
  1 Tablespoon vegetable broth powder of choice
  1 teaspoon salt
  1 teaspoon olive oil
  2 Tablespoons Bragg's Liquid Aminos
  ½ teaspoon onion powder
  ½ teaspoon garlic powder
  ½ teaspoon thyme
  1 onion, diced
  1 teaspoon parsley flakes, dry
  1/8 teaspoon cayenne pepper, optional

Bring ingredients to a simmer over medium heat, and then add:

continued

4 cups cooked brown rice
2 cups chunk TVP® soaked and lightly chopped
   or 2 cups gluten cut into pieces

Cook soup for 10 minutes. Add more water in necessary, and then serve.

Hearty Beef Style Stew

4 large potatoes
2 stalks celery, sliced diagonally
2 carrots, peeled and sliced diagonally
1 onion, cut into cubes
1 qt. water

Put above ingredients into a pot and cook over medium eat until potatoes are slightly tender, drain the water out of the pot and then add,

1 lb. beef style gluten, cut into chunks
1 qt. stewed tomatoes
1 cup water
1 T. vegetable broth powder
1-2 t. sea salt
1 t. Italian seasoning
2-3 T. Bragg's liquid aminos
1 t. onion powder
1 t. garlic powder
Dash of cayenne pepper

Cook until ingredients are well heated and then serve.

VEGETARIAN ENTRÉES

Sister, Sister Veggie Couscous Loaf

My sister Danielle and I had to prepare a meal for a rather large group of people. I had planned veggie burgers on the menu, but we decided against it because we thought it time consuming, so we created this recipe on the spot and hoped for the best. Everyone thoroughly enjoyed this new recipe and said it tasted like real meat loaf. Try it for yourself and see if you like it!

2 cups cooked couscous, hot
2 cups ground bread
1½ cups walnuts, ground
1 small onion, diced
1 green pepper, diced
1 teaspoon onion powder
1 teaspoon garlic powder
2 teaspoons salt
1 Tablespoons Italian seasoning
5 T. Bragg's Liquid Aminos
1 Tablespoon Seitenbacher Vegetable Broth
    Mix, or vegetable broth of choice
2 Tablespoons nutritional yeast flakes
1 (6 ounce) can tomato paste
Water to moisten

Combine first thirteen ingredients together in a large mixing bowl, stir well, then add water, just enough to make the mixture moist, not soggy. Press mixture into a loaf pan greased with tahini. Place in the oven at 350°. Bake for 45 minutes, remove from oven and spread **Hot'n Spicy Sauce** (*below*) on top of loaf. Place loaf back in the oven and bake for another 20–30 minutes. Cut loaf when cooled.

Sweet Hot'n Spicy Sauce (for top of loaf)

1 (6 ounce) can tomato paste
2 teaspoons salt
½ teaspoon cayenne pepper
1 teaspoon onion powder
¼ cup honey
2–3 Tablespoons molasses
Water enough to make saucy

Mix all ingredients together in a bowl, stir well, and then use over loaf.

Browned Tofu

Many have said that this recipe taste like chicken!

1 pound tofu, extra firm
3 Tablespoons tahini
1 teaspoon salt
1 teaspoon onion powder
1 teaspoon garlic powder
1 teaspoon Italian seasoning or oregano, optional

Slice tofu into pieces and put into a non-stick pan. Add tahini, salt, onion and garlic powder and herbs. Lightly toss until tofu becomes coated with tahini and seasonings. Brown tofu over medium heat on range top. Toss gently. When tofu starts to brown a little, add:

3 Tablespoons Bragg's Liquid Aminos

Quickly toss tofu after liquid aminos has been added. When you pour the liquid aminos onto the hot pan it will steam and you don't want to lose the flavor. Continue browning the tofu until it takes on a golden brown color, then use as desired.

continued

Variation: Tofu can be browned with onions and peppers. Vegetables can also be browned instead of tofu. You can replace the tofu with any of the following vegetables, 1 large eggplant peeled and cubed, or 3 fresh zucchini sliced or cubed, or 5 medium boiled potatoes, cubed and follow the recipe as directed for tofu.

Pimiento Cheese Rice Casserole

4 cups brown rice, cooked (*see recipe, p. 131*)
1 small onion, sliced
1 green pepper, sliced
1 Tablespoon tahini or water
1½ cups green peas, fresh or frozen
1 recipe **Browned Tofu** (*see recipe, p. 96*)

Put cooked rice into a bowl and set aside. Put sliced onion and pepper into a non-stick pan and sauté with the water or tahini for about 5 minutes, then add to the rice. Add peas and tofu to rice and stir. Then add:

1 recipe **Pimiento Cheese Sauce** (*see recipe, p. 54*)

Stir in pimiento cheese sauce, put mixture into an appropriate size glass casserole pan, sprinkle with breadcrumbs and bake in the oven at 350° for 30–40 minutes.

Variation: Fresh diced zucchini can be added to this recipe.

Yields approximately 4–5 servings.

Right Side Up Pizza Cornbread

1 recipe of **Cornbread batter** (*see recipe*)

Spread batter one inch thick onto a cookie sheet greased with tahini. Bake as directed. Let cool thoroughly. Set aside. Assemble together:

2 cups pizza sauce of choice
1 recipe **Browned Tofu** (*see recipe, p. 96*)
1 small onion, sliced
1 cup black olives, sliced
1 green pepper, sliced
1 cup **Pimiento Cheese Sauce** (*see recipe, p. 54*)
1 Tablespoon dried oregano

Layer ingredients on top of cornbread. Put the sauce on first, add the tofu, next the onion and pepper, and then the olives. Drizzle on the pimiento cheese, and then sprinkle on the oregano. Place in the oven at 350° for 15–20 minutes. Serve.

Variation: To make Upside Down Pizza Cornbread, put pizza sauce, browned tofu, onion, black olives, green pepper, pimiento cheese and oregano on the bottom of a casserole dish. Pour cornbread batter over top until covered. Place green pepper rings on top of cornbread batter for garnish. Place immediately in a pre-heated oven at 350°, and bake for 30–45 minutes.

Yields approximately 6–8 servings, depending on slice size.

Shepherd's Pie

>1 pound bag frozen mixed vegetables (find a
>   mix that has broccoli, cauliflower, and car-
>   rots in it)

Lightly steam veggies in a pot, just enough to thaw and melt
the ice crystals from the frozen vegetables. Put vegetables
into a bowl and add:

>½ recipe **Browned tofu** (*see recipe, p. 96*)
>½ recipe **Cashew gravy** (*see recipe, p. 57*) or 1
>   recipe **Turkey Style gravy**, (*see recipe, p. 49*)

Stir together the vegetables, tofu, and gravy and put
at the bottom of a casserole dish, set aside and make;

>a double recipe of **Mashed Potatoes** (*see recipe,
>   p. 81*)

Spread mashed potatoes evenly over top of vegetables. Bake
at 350° for 30–45 minutes.

Yields approximately 4–5 servings.

Easy Vegetarian Lasagna

>1 (10 ounce) box DeBoles artichoke lasagna
>   noodles (**don't cook!**)
>1 recipe **Browned Tofu** (*see recipe, p. 96*)
>2 zuchini squash, sliced or shredded or 1
>   (10 ounce) bag frozen chopped broccoli,
>   thawed
>3 cups **Pimiento Cheese Sauce** (*see recipe, p.
>   54*)
>2 quarts tomato sauce of choice
>1 (6 ounce) can black olives
>Italian seasoning or oregano

continued

Assemble lasagna by alternating layers as follows:

Put 2 cups of tomato sauce on the bottom of a deep casserole dish, next lay 4–6 dry noodles down flat, spread 2 cups of sauce on top of noodles, add ½ the tofu, ½ the squash or broccoli, 1 cup of cheese sauce, ½ the black olives. Repeat starting with noodles, sauce, etc. End with noodles on top, spread remaining sauce on top of noodles, and drizzle on the last cup of cheese sauce, sprinkle lightly Italian seasoning or oregano. Cover casserole dish with foil, seal edges as tightly as possible. Bake at 300 for 1 hour or until noodles can be pierced with a fork. Remove foil, place back in the oven at 350° for 10 minutes to dry the top.

Variation: Use **Onion & Herb flat Bread** (*see recipe, p. 42*) in the layers instead of lasagna noodles. Use slightly less tomato sauce so that chapattis don't become too soggy, and bake uncovered at 350° for 30–45 minutes.

Yields approximately 5–6 servings.

Crispy Breaded Tofu Sticks

Best eaten hot from the oven.

> 1 pound extra firm tofu

Slice tofu into ¼ inch slices, then cut lengthwise into sticks.

> 2 cups dry bread crumbs of choice, seasoned

Place tofu into the bread crumbs and cover until well coated. Put onto a cookie sheet (ungreased) and bake at 400° for 15 minutes on one side, turn over and bake for 10–15 more minutes or until golden brown and crispy. Dip tofu sticks in ketchup or any dip or sauce of choice.

Spicy Tofu Dish

> 2 cups water
> 1 Tablespoon Seitenbacher Vegetable Broth
>   Mix
> 2 Tablespoons Bragg's Liquid Aminos
> 1 teaspoon onion powder
> 1 teaspoon garlic powder
> ¼ teaspoon Italian seasoning
> 1/8 teaspoon cayenne pepper or red pepper
>   flakes

Put all ingredients into a saucepan and place over medium heat. Add:

> ½ pound extra firm tofu, cubed

Bring to a slow simmer and continue for 5–8 minutes to allow flavor to soak into the tofu, then prepare in a small bowl:

> 2 Tablespoons cornstarch
> 4 Tablespoons water

Mix together cornstarch and water and pour slowly while stirring into tofu and broth in the saucepan. Cook until thickened. Serve over cooked brown rice or pasta.

Yields approximately 2–3 servings.

Simple Vegetable Stir Fry

Prepare 1 recipe of **Browned Tofu (*see recipe, p. 96*)**, and then add to the pan:

> 1 bag frozen stir-fry vegetable mix of choice

Cover tofu and vegetables with a lid for 5 minutes, until the frost melts from the veggies. Remove lid, turn the heat down low, and make the gravy. In a glass jar add:

continued

1 cup water
¼ cup Bragg's Liquid Aminos
3–4 Tablespoons honey
2 Tablespoons cornstarch or tapioca starch
1 teaspoon onion powder
½ teaspoon garlic powder
1–2 teaspoons salt

Put a lid on the jar and shake up its contents until well blended, then pour over the tofu and vegetables and cook until gravy thickens. Serve vegetable stir-fry over cooked brown rice or cooked pasta of choice.

Yields approximately 4 servings.

Haystacks

Haystacks are a complete, satisfying easy to eat taco! Children love'em and adults too!

Haystack #1

corn or tortilla chips of choice (fat free, baked
    preferred)
Spicy 3 Bean Chili (*see recipe, p. 103*)
shredded lettuce, iceberg or romaine
diced tomato
diced onion
sliced black olives

Haystack #2

corn or tortilla chips of choice (fat free, baked
preferred)
Spicy 3 Bean Chili (*see recipe, p. 103*)
diced cucumber
cubed avocado
diced tomato
sliced black olives
diced onion

Haystack #3

corn or tortilla chips of choice (fat free, baked
preferred)
Spicy 3 Bean Chili (*see recipe, p. 103*)
diced cucumber
diced red onion
sliced olives

Haystack Assembly:

Make a pot of chili, pre-cut all veggies and put into separate
dishes. Make **Pimiento Cheese Sauce** (*see recipe, p. 54*) or
Tofu Cashew Sour Crème (*see recipe, p. 53*) and pre-chill in
the refrigerator. To assemble haystack, take a desired amount
of chips and crush lightly on a plate. Scoop desired amount
of chili over chips, then put on veggies in whatever order you
desire and top with Pimiento Cheese or Tofu Cashew Sour
Cream. **Enjoy!**

Spicy 3 Bean Chili

1 can kidney beans
1 can black beans
1 can pinto beans
¼ cup TVP® granules (dry)
1 cup tomato paste
¼ cup honey

continued

    1 teaspoon onion powder
    1 teaspoon garlic powder
    1 teaspoon salt
    ½ teaspoon cumin
    ½ teaspoon oregano
    1 pinch cayenne pepper
    1 teaspoon Italian seasoning
    ½ cup water or more if needed

Put all ingredients into a small pot, stir and cook over medium heat for approximately 10 minutes or until bubbling. Serve as desired.

Noodle Cabbage Stroganoff

    1 box cooked DeBole's® ribbons or spirals
    3 cups cooked cabbage (drain off the cooking water)
    1 carrot, shredded
    1 cup fresh or frozen peas
    1 recipe **Browned Tofu** (*see recipe, p. 96*)
    1 recipe **Cashew Gravy** (*see recipe, p. 57*)

Mix all ingredients together in a mixing bowl, put into a casserole dish of suitable size, sprinkle the top with bread crumbs and place into a 350° oven uncovered for 25–30 minutes.

Yields approximately 4 servings.

Stuffed Zucchini

This is a good recipe for using up those overgrown zucchini squash in your garden.

> 1–2 large overgrown zucchini squash (make
> sure the outer skin is not too tough or the
> inside flesh too woody in texture.)

Wash zucchini, and cut into 2-inch thick circles. Hollow out the seeded middle with a knife. Fill hollowed out zucchini centers with **Sister, Sister Couscous Veggie Loaf** mixture (*see recipe, p. 95*), or any other favorite patty or loaf mix. Put 2 cups of **Cashew Gravy** (*see recipe, p. 57*) on the bottom of a casserole dish. Place filled zucchini circles down in the pan flat. Pour more gravy on top of zucchini and sprinkle with thyme. Cover pan with a lid or foil and place in the oven at 350°. Bake for 45 minutes to an hour, or until zucchini is soft and can be pierced with a fork. Serve.

Variation: Your favorite tomato sauce can be used instead of the Cashew Gravy and oregano can be sprinkled on top instead of thyme.

Stuffed Zucchini Boats

> 3 small zucchini squash

Wash zucchini, cut off the ends, then cut down the middle lengthwise. Scrape out the seeds. Set aside and prepare filling.

Filling:

> 2 cups cooked brown rice
> ½ pound tofu, mashed
> 1 teaspoon salt
> 1 teaspoon onion powder
> 1 teaspoon garlic powder
> 1 teaspoon Italian seasoning

continued

1 teaspoon Seitenbacher Vegetable Broth Mix
pinch cayenne pepper

Combine all ingredients together in a mixing bowl and mix well. Stuff zucchini boats with filling. Put 3 cups of tomato sauce of choice on the bottom of a casserole dish, and then place zucchini boats in the pan with the sauce. Cover the top of boats with more sauce, and then drizzle the top with **Pimiento Cheese Sauce (*See recipe, p. 54*)** Finish with a sprinkle of oregano. Cover casserole dish with a lid or foil and place in the oven at 350°. Bake for 45 minutes or until the zucchini is soft and can be pierced with a fork.

Yields approximately 6 servings.

Variation: Use green bell pepper halves instead of the zucchini. Wash and cut peppers in half, scrape out the seeds and stuff with the filling, then continue the recipe as directed.

Spaghetti n' Cheese Casserole

1 box spaghetti of choice (wheat, artichoke,
    rice, corn, etc.)

Cook spaghetti according to the directions on the box. Drain, rinse, and put into a mixing bowl. Add:

1 recipe **Browned Tofu (*See recipe*)**

Sautée together:

1 onion, sliced
1 green pepper, sliced

(Sautee in 1–2 Tablespoons water in a non-stick pan, then add to the bowl with the cooked spaghetti.)

Stir in 4–6 cups of your favorite tomato sauce.

continued

Mix spaghetti, tofu, onion, pepper, and sauce together well, then put into a casserole dish. Set aside and make:

> 1 recipe **Pimiento Cheese Sauce (*see recipe, p. 54*)**

Spread 1–2 cups of pimiento cheese on top of spaghetti evenly. Lightly sprinkle the top with oregano. Bake in a 350° oven for 30–40 minutes.

Yields approximately 4–5 servings.

Walnut Oat Burgers (*Revised Recipe*)

In a small pot add:

> 5 Tablespoons Bragg's Liquid Aminos
> 1¾ cups water
> 3 Tablespoons dried onion flakes

Bring pot contents to a boil over medium heat. While liquid broth is coming to a boil, start mixing together the dry ingredients. In a medium size bowl add:

> 2 cups rolled oats
> 1 cup walnuts, finely ground
> 1 Tablespoon Seitenbacher Vegetable Broth
>   Mix
> 1/8 teaspoon salt, opt.
> 1 teaspoon garlic powder
> 1 teaspoon Italian seasoning
> Pinch of cayenne pepper

Once liquid broth in the pot has come to a boil, turn heat off. Gradually add the dry mixture into the pot with the liquid broth, stir briefly, put a lid on the pot and let stand for 15–20 minutes, or until all the liquid is adsorbed. Let cool, then form into patties. Place patties on a greased cookie sheet.

continued

Bake at 350° for 30–35 minutes. Turn patties over half way through baking time so that both sides get browned.
Serve with favorite dressing, dip or ketchup.

Makes 8 burgers.

Gluten Pepper Steak

> 2 cups gluten, sliced
> 1 teaspoon olive oil
> 1 green bell pepper, sliced into strips
> 　　(*you can also use a variety of colored peppers
> 　　to enhance the color of this dish*)
> 1 small onion, sliced

Add gluten to a non-stick pan with olive oil and the sliced pepper. Brown over medium heat for a few minutes.

To make gravy: mix 1½ cups of the gluten broth with 1 Tablespoon cornstarch. Stir together well and pour into the pan with the gluten. Cook until gravy thickens.

Serve over brown rice or pasta. **Delicious!**

Stuffed Jumbo Shells

12 jumbo pasta shells of choice

In a pot of boiling water add dry pasta shells, cook just until shells are soft enough to pull open about 8–10 minutes. Set shells aside in cold water and prepare filling. In a bowl add:

1 pound tofu, extra firm
1 teaspoon garlic powder
1 teaspoon onion powder
1–2 teaspoons salt
2 Tablespoons lemon juice
1 Tablespoon parsley flakes
2 Tablespoons **Mock Parmesan Cheese Substitute** (*see recipe, p. 132*)

Put tofu into a bowl and mash with a fork or masher, stir in remaining ingredients. Set aside. In a casserole dish spread on the bottom:

2 cups tomato sauce (favorite sauce of choice)

Stuff shells with filling and line the pan with the tomato sauce, place in the pan with the open side of the shell facing up. Cover the top of shells with more tomato sauce. Drizzle **Pimiento Cheese Sauce** (*see recipe, p. 54*) on top and sprinkle on a generous amount of Mock Parmesan Cheese Substitute and a dash of Italian seasoning or oregano. Cover pan with foil and bake at 350° for 25–30 minutes, uncover pan and brown the top of casserole for 5–8 minutes.

Wheat Meat

Easy gluten recipe

In a mixing bowl add:

> 1½ cups vital wheat gluten flour
> ¼ cup whole wheat flour

Mix both flours together thoroughly, then with a wire whip stir in:

> 1½ cups water

Mixture will quickly become stiff rubbery dough. Knead for a few seconds, then cut dough into chunks, strips, or steaks and drop into a pot of rapidly boiling broth. Cook gluten at a steady simmer for 1–2 hours. Gluten will puff up and become meaty. The whole lump of dough can be boiled to make a roast for slicing.

Gluten makes a wonderful meat substitute and can be used in many vegetarian recipes. Gluten can be kept frozen for 3–6 months.

Broth

In a large pot add:

> 12 cups water
> ¾ cup Bragg's Liquid Aminos
> 3 teaspoons salt
> 2 Tablespoons Seitenbacher Vegetable Broth
>   Mix
> 2 teaspoons Italian seasoning
> 2 teaspoons garlic powder
> 2 teaspoons onion powder

continued

Bring broth to a rapid boil over medium heat. Add gluten dough pieces. Keep a lid on the pot while cooking or gluten will not cook through to the inside.

Orange Marmalade Glazed Tofu

Put a 1 pound cake of extra firm tofu in the freezer and freeze for at least 12–24 hours. Remove from freezer to thaw. Thawing tofu takes time, so you may want to thaw it a day before use. Squeeze the excess water from the tofu and cut it into cubes. Brown tofu following the instructions for **Browned Tofu (*See recipe, p. 96*)**. Put tofu into a baking dish and set aside. In a non-stick pan add:

> ½ red pepper, sliced into long thin strips
> 1 small onion, sliced
> 1 teaspoon olive oil

Sautee peppers and onions in the olive oil until slightly browned. Mix sautéed onion and pepper into the browned tofu and set aside. In a small saucepan mix together ingredients for the glaze:

> ½ cup orange marmalade jelly, sugar free
> ¼ cup honey
> ½ cup orange juice or water
> 1 Tablespoon sesame seeds

Heat glaze over medium heat until glaze is thin and syrupy. Pour glaze evenly over tofu and toss lightly. Put tofu into the oven at 350° and bake for ½ hour covered. Uncover pan and bake for another 15–20 minutes. Check tofu periodically and baste with a baster, covering the dry exposed pieces of tofu with the glaze juices. When tofu is done most of the glaze juices should be absorbed by the tofu.

Rice 'n Beans

4 cups water
1–2 teaspoon annatto powder or you can sub-
    stitute the annatto with ½ teaspoon tur-
    meric powder or omit both. (The annatto or
    turmeric gives the rice color.)
3 Tablespoon lemon juice
1 teaspoon sea salt
2 cups brown rice

Put water, annatto, lemon juice, and salt into a pot and bring
to a boil over medium heat. Add rice and continue to boil
rapidly for 5 minutes, and then turn down the heat and cover
the pot with a lid until the contents in the pot gently simmer.
Cook rice for 1 hour, or until all the liquid in the pot has been
absorbed by the rice. Turn heat off, fluff up the rice and set
aside. In a non-stick skillet add:

1 can kidney beans
½ green pepper, diced
3 cloves fresh garlic, minced
1 Tablespoons olive oil, extra virgin
½ teaspoon onion powder
Dash of cayenne pepper
Salt to taste

Heat beans over medium heat for about 5 minutes or until
the peppers become soft, and then add the rice. Cook for another 10 minutes and then serve.

Almond Loaf

2 cups almonds, ground
2 cups cooked brown rice
¼ cup quick oats
3 cups cubed bread, wheat
¼ cup tahini
1 small onion, chopped
1 stalk celery, diced
1–2 Tablespoons Braggs Liquid Aminos
1 Tablespoon vegetable broth powder
1 teaspoon onion powder
1 teaspoon garlic powder
2 teaspoons thyme
1 teaspoon sea salt
1 cup soy milk

Combine all ingredients together in a mixing bowl, mix well. Press mixture into a oiled loaf pan or square baking dish. Bake at 350° for 35 minutes.

Serve with favorite gravy.

Jasmine Rice Burgers

2 cups cooked whole grain Jasmine rice, hot
1 cup bread crumbs
1 cup walnuts, finely ground
1 teaspoon Italian seasoning
½ teaspoon thyme
1 teaspoon salt
1 Tablespoon Bragg's Liquid Aminos
2 teaspoons Seitenbacher Vegetable Broth Mix
1 small onion, chopped
½ red pepper, diced
Dash of cayenne pepper, optional
A little water to moisten

continued

Mix all ingredients together in a mixing bowl, mix well. Be careful not to add too much water, you want the mixture to be moist not soggy. Form mixture into burgers and place on an oiled cookie sheet. Bake at 350° for approximately 15–20 minutes on one side. Remove from the oven and flip burgers over. Bake for another 8–10 minutes.

HEALTHY DESSERTS

Plum Crumb Pie

2 cans of plums, pitted (use 30 oz. size)
1 cup honey
1 Tablespoon lemon juice
2 teaspoons pure vanilla extract

Put all ingredients into a pot and cook over medium heat until bubbling, and then add:

3 Tablespoons water
3 Tablespoons cornstarch

Mix water and cornstarch together in a separate bowl, and pour into plums while gently stirring. Cook filling until thickened, and pour into an unbaked pie shell. The **Cashew Wheat Pie Crust** (*see recipe, p. 122*), works well for this recipe.

Plum Crumb Topping

½ cup quick oats
1 teaspoon coriander
1/3 cup walnuts
1/3 cup whole wheat pastry flour
½ cup date sugar
¼ teaspoon salt
2 Tablespoons tahini

Put all ingredients into a food processor; blend until fine and well mixed. Put crumb topping on top of pie and pat down with hands or a spoon. Place pie in the oven at 350° and bake for 30 minutes. Let pie cool before slicing. This pie can also be made with apple filling to make an apple crumb pie.

Lemon Poppy Seed Cake

2¾ cups whole wheat pastry flour
1 cup honey
2 Tablespoons poppy seeds
1 teaspoon salt
1 teaspoon pure lemon extract or oil
½ cup tahini
1/8 teaspoon turmeric powder

Put all ingredients into a mixing bowl and stir together well, then pour in together:

1¼ cups soymilk
½ cup 3% hydrogen peroxide

Mix together quickly with a wire whip, and pour batter into a cake pan greased with tahini. Put cake into a pre-heated oven at 350°, and bake for 30–40 minutes.

Serving suggestion: Serve Lemon Poppy Seed Cake with a strawberry sauce.

Tofu Cheese Cake

This recipe taste very much like real cheesecake.

2 boxes of Mori-Nu® tofu, extra firm silken, lite
1 cup honey
2 teaspoons pure vanilla extract
1 teaspoon butter extract
½ teaspoon salt
2 Tablespoons cornstarch

Put all ingredients into an electric blender and blend until smooth. Set aside and make granola walnut crust.

Granola Walnut Crust for Cheesecake

> 1 cup granola (Use granola of choice without
>   raisins)
> ½ cup walnuts

Put granola and walnuts into a food processor and blend until fine. Then pat mixture evenly with hands on the bottom of a pie pan or quiche pan. Pour tofu cheesecake filling over top of granola crust and bake in the oven at 300° for 45 minutes to an hour. Cheesecake will develop cracks in the oven, but that is OK. Let cool then top with fruit topping of choice. Refrigerate.

Cashew Vanilla Pudding

> 1 cup cashews
> ½ cup honey
> 1 Tablespoon pure vanilla extract
> ½ teaspoon salt
> 3–4 Tablespoons cornstarch
> 4 cups water or Edensoy milk original

Put all ingredients into an electric blender and blend until very smooth, about 5 minutes. Pour into a pot and cook over medium heat while stirring constantly until thickened. Refrigerate to set.

4 tablespoons of carob powder can be added to this recipe to make carob pudding.

Banana Crème Pie

Have ready 1 pre-baked **Cashew Wheat Pie Crust** (*see recipe, p. 122*).

2 ripe bananas

Slice banana and arrange slices on the bottom of baked piecrust, set aside. Make one recipe of **Cashew Vanilla Pudding** (*See recipe, 117*). 1 teaspoon of banana extract may be substituted for the vanilla extract or both may be used. Pour pudding over the sliced bananas, sprinkle the top with unsweetened shredded coconut, and refrigerate to set.

Oatmeal Peanut Butter Cookies

5 cups quick oats
1 cup shredded coconut, unsweetened
¾ cup walnuts, chopped
½ cup raisins
1 teaspoon salt

Combine together all dry ingredients in a large mixing bowl, set aside. In another bowl add:

1 cup honey
1 cup tahini
½ cup peanut butter
1 teaspoon pure vanilla extract

Stir together well, and then mix the wet ingredients with the dry mixture. Mix well, until mixture becomes sticky. Form mixture into walnut size balls; place on a cookie sheet and smash with fingers or a spoon. Bake at 350° for 15–20 minutes. Let cool.

Vacation Apple Bars

I originally created this recipe while on vacation with my family in Florida.

> 4 cups quick oats
> 1 cup shredded coconut, unsweetened
> 1 cup whole wheat pastry flour
> ½ cup date sugar
> ½ cup tahini
> 1 teaspoon vanilla extract
> 1 teaspoon coriander
> ½ teaspoon nutmeg
> 1–2 Tablespoons honey

Put all ingredients together in a mixing bowl, and mix with hands, rubbing mixture together between hands to crush the oats. Set aside and make apple filling.

Apple Filling:

> 6 green apples, or any variety of hard apple
> ½ cup honey
> 1 teaspoon vanilla extract
> 1 Tablespoon lemon juice

Peel and slice apples, put into a pot and add the honey, vanilla, and lemon juice. Cook over medium heat until apples are soft, but not mushy, then add:

> 1–2 Tablespoons cornstarch mixed with 3
>   Tablespoons water

Pour cornstarch and water mixture into the pot with the apples and stir gently. Continue cooking apples until filling has thickened.

continued

Assemble Apple Bars:

Cover the bottom of a small cookie sheet with half of the oat mixture. Next spread on the apple filling evenly. Then cover with the rest of the oat mixture, and pack down with hands. Place the bars in the oven at 350° and bake for 25–35 minutes. Let cool before cutting into bars.

Pumpkin Pie

> 2 (15 ounce) cans pumpkin
> 1 cup honey
> 2 teaspoons vanilla extract
> 1 teaspoon nutmeg

Put pumpkin, honey, vanilla, and nutmeg into a bowl. Set aside and make the cream.

Cream:

> 1 cup cashews
> ¼ cup cornstarch
> 1 teaspoon salt
> ¾–1 cup water

Put all ingredients into a blender and blend until smooth and creamy. Pour cream into the bowl with the pumpkin mixture. Stir well and pour pumpkin filling into an unbaked pie shell. Put into the oven at 300° and bake for 1 hour. Chill for several hours and serve.

Pineapple Upside Down Cake

> 1 (20 ounce) can pineapple, unsweetened
>   (crushed or tidbits)
> ¼ cup honey

Open can pineapple and thoroughly drain off the juice. Put into a saucepan with the honey and caramelize over medium heat, until pineapple becomes candy-like. Put caramelized pineapple on the bottom of a cake pan greased with tahini. Set aside. In a mixing bowl, combine:

> 1 ¼ cup whole wheat pastry flour
> ½ teaspoon salt
> ¾ cup honey

Set dry ingredients aside. In a blender add:

> ½ cup soymilk
> 1 Tablespoon vanilla extract
> ½ cup tahini

Briefly blend together in the blender, the soymilk, vanilla, and the tahini. Stop blender and pour in:

> 1/3 cup 3% peroxide

Stir peroxide in with a spoon, (Do not turn blender back on) and then pour blender contents into the bowl with the flour, salt, and honey. Mix together quickly and well. Pour batter over the pineapple in the cake pan. Immediately place in a preheated oven at 350°, and bake for 50 minutes or until a toothpick comes out clean after inserting it in the center of the cake. Let cool, then frost or glaze as desired.

Peanut Butter Cookies

    1 cup peanut butter, smooth
    2/3 cup honey
    1 teaspoon vanilla extract
    ½ teaspoon salt
    1 cup whole wheat pastry flour or soy flour

In a mixing bowl combine peanut butter, honey, vanilla, and salt. Stir together, and then add flour slowly. Do not over mix cookie dough or it will become oily and crumbly. Roll dough into balls; place on a cookie sheet and smash with a fork or spoon. Put into the oven on top rack at 350° and bake for 10–15 minutes or until lightly browned. Let cool before removing from the cookie sheet.

Cashew Wheat Pie Crust

    1 cup cashews
    1 teaspoon salt
    2 Tablespoons tahini
    1 cup ice cold water

Put the above ingredients into a blender and blend until smooth. Pour contents of blender into a mixing bowl and add:

    2–2 ½ cups whole wheat pastry flour

Add flour slowly until mixture becomes a soft dough. Do not over mix or knead dough too much or it will become tough and elastic, which will result in a hard pie crust once baked.

Use as desired. This dough can be kept frozen in the freezer for 3–6 months.

Mom's Vanilla Cake

> 3 cups whole wheat pastry flour
> 1 cup honey
> 1 teaspoon salt

Put the flour, fructose, and salt in a mixing bowl and set aside. In an electric blender add:

> 1 cup soymilk (Edensoy original is preferable)
> 1 cup tahini
> 3 teaspoons vanilla extract
> 2 teaspoons coconut extract

Turn blender on and blend for 1 minute. Turn blender off and add:

> ½ cup 3% hydrogen peroxide

Gently stir in peroxide with a spoon. (Do not turn blender on again). Pour blender contents into the mixing bowl with the flour, honey, and salt. Quickly stir and pour batter into a cake pan smeared with tahini. Place in the oven at 350° for 35 minutes, or until toothpick inserted into the center of the cake comes out clean. Let cool, then glaze or frost.

Basic Plain Cake

In a mixing bowl add:

> 1½ cups whole wheat pastry flour
> 1 cup brown rice flour
> ½ cup pecan or almond meal
> 1 teaspoon salt

Stir together and set bowl aside. In a blender begin adding the following ingredients:

continued

1½ cup soy, rice, or almond milk
½ cup tahini
1 cup honey
2 teaspoon pure vanilla extract,
   alcohol free
1 teaspoon lemon oil or extract
1 teaspoon almond extract,
   alcohol free

Set blender aside. In a small pot add:

1 heaping Tablespoon flaxseed, ground
3 Tablespoons water

Cook flaxseed and water together for a few seconds over low heat until mixture becomes slimy, and then add to the blender with the other ingredients. Blend for about 1 minute until mixture becomes foamy and frothy. Pour this mixture into the bowl together with,

½ cup 3% hydrogen peroxide

Stir together quickly with a wire whip and pour batter into an oiled cake pan. Place immediately into an oven preheated at 350° degrees. Bake for 40–45 minutes. Let cool before frosting.

Tofu Carob Frosting

1 pound cake tofu, extra firm
½ cup carob powder, dark roasted
1 teaspoon vanilla extract
½ teaspoon salt
½ cup honey
1 cup soy milk

Put all ingredients into a blender and blend until smooth and creamy. Add more soy milk if necessary. Use frosting as desired.

Honey Spice Sticky Buns

Make one recipe of **Tahini Yeast Biscuit dough**, (*see recipe, p. 32*). Roll dough out into an oblong triangle, approximately 8 inches wide and 12 inches long, and about ¼ inch thick, then spread with:

> 1/3 cup honey
> 3 teaspoons **Cinnamon Substitute**, (*see recipe, p. 132*)

Roll up from the long side into a jelly roll like log. Pinch underside of dough together to keep closed. With a sharp serated knife, slice roll into ¼ inch slices. Lay sticky buns flat in a pan (glass or steel) greased with tahini. Let buns proof for 10–15 minutes, then place in a pre-heated oven at 325° and bake for 25–30 minutes or until lightly browned. Let cool then glaze.

Variation: To make Pineapple Bottom Danish, open a can of unsweetened pineapple slices, drain juice into a small pot. Lay pineapple slices down on the bottom of a glass casserole dish. Sweeten juice with honey and a little vanilla extract to taste. Bring juice to a simmer over medium heat and thicken juice with a mixture of 1 level Tablespoon cornstarch and 3 teaspoons water. Pour cornstarch mixture into simmering juice while stirring to prevent lumps. Cook until thickened and pour syrup over sliced pineapple. Place slices of unbaked sticky buns on top of each slice of pineapple. Let buns proof and bake for the recommended time. Let cool then glaze.

Vanilla Cookie Cutter Cut-Outs

> ½ cup tahini
> ¼ cup honey
> 1 teaspoon vanilla extract

Put tahini, honey, and vanilla into a mixing bowl and set aside. In a small pot add:

> 2 teaspoons flaxseed, ground
> 2 Tablespoons water

Place over medium heat and let simmer until mixture becomes slimy like egg yolk, then add flaxseed mixture to the bowl with the other ingredients and stir together. In a separate bowl mix together:

> 2 cups whole wheat pastry flour
> 1 teaspoon Ener-G Baking Powder (level)

Mix flour and baking powder together, and then add slowly to the contents of the mixing bowl to form a soft dough. Wrap dough in wax paper and put into the freezer for 20 minutes to a ½ hour. (Cookie dough should be firm enough to handle). Roll dough out and cut into shapes with cookie cutters, place on a cookie sheet. Bake at 350° for 5–6 minutes or until lightly browned. Place cookies on a cooling wrack to cool.

Strawberry Orange Fruitcicles

1 cup orange juice concentrate
15 strawberries, fresh or frozen
honey to taste
¼ teaspoon almond extract

Put all ingredients into a blender and blend until smooth. Pour mixture into a popsicle mold maker. Freeze until hard, then enjoy!

Grape Slushy

2 cups grape juice, unsweetened
honey to taste
½ teaspoon almond extract
14 ice cubes

Put all ingredients into a blender (A Vita-Mix® works best) and blend until smooth. Serve immediately.

Yields 2 servings.

Whipped Coconut Crème

In a blender add:

2 cups boiling water
2 Tablespoons Agar powder

Blend the first two ingredients together for 30 seconds, and then add:

1 (13.5 ounce) can coconut milk (premium grade)
½ cup cashews
3 teaspoons lecithin granules
¾ cup sweetener of choice
1 teaspoon almond extract

continued

Blend until smooth, pour into a container and refrigerate until set or firm. Put cream into a bowl and whip with a hand mixer until fluffy and smooth.

Use as you would whip cream.

Strawberry Shortcake

Strawberry filling:

In a pot add,

> 1 pint of strawberries, fresh or frozen
> ½ cup honey
> 1 tsp. vanilla extract

Bring strawberries to a simmer over medium heat. In a small bowl mix together

> 1–2 Tbs. cornstarch
> 3–4 Tbs. water

Stir cornstarch and water together and pour slowly into the simmering strawberries while stirring constantly to prevent lumps. Cook until thickened. Refrigerate to chill. Make a recipe of Quick Peroxide Biscuits. Let biscuits cool and then split in half. Place one scoop of strawberry filling on the bottom half of biscuit and cover with the other biscuit half. Top with another scoop of strawberry filling and a dollop of **Whipped Coconut Crème** (**See recipe, p. 127**).

Yields approximately 4 strawberry shortcakes.

SANDWICH IDEAS
&
MISCELLANEOUS RECIPES

Grilled Pimiento Cheese Sandwiches

Ingredients needed for 1 sandwich:

> 2 slices whole wheat bread
> tahini
> **Pimiento Cheese Sauce**, (*see recipe, p. 54*)
> 1 thick slice of tomato
> Dash of salt

To Assemble:

Spread a very thin layer of tahini on one side of each slice of bread. Next spread Pimiento Cheese Sauce on one side of both slices of bread (the side without tahini on it). Put tomato on one slice of bread, directly on top of the cheese. Sprinkle a dash of salt over tomato and put the two slices of bread together. Brown sandwich on both sides (the sides with the tahini exposed) in a non-stick pan or on an indoor grill.

Raw Veggie Tofu Sandwich

Ingredients needed for 1 sandwich:

> 2 slices whole wheat or rye bread
> **Creamy Cucumber Dressing**, (*see recipe, p. 52*)
> Fresh, extra firm tofu, sliced into ¼ inch bricks
> Sliced tomato
> Sliced avocado
> Alfalfa sprouts
> 1 sliced red onion

 continued

To Assemble:

Toast bread and spread Cucumber Dressing on both sides. Next, lay the tofu slices, then the vegetables in order on top of one slice of bread, then cover sandwich with the last slice of bread. **Enjoy!**

Spicy Avocado Sandwich

Ingredients needed for 1 sandwich

> 2 slices of bread
> 4 slices of avocado, cut lengthwise
> **Creamy Cucumber Dressing**, (*see recipe, p. 52*)
> Salt to taste
> Dash of cayenne pepper
> 1 slice of red onion, optional

To Assemble:

Toast bread and spread dressing on each slice. Lay slices of avocado on one half and sprinkle with salt and cayenne pepper. Next add the onion, and then cover with the last slice of bread.

Fluffy Cooked Brown Rice

Does your brown rice come out sticky, gooey, and starchy? Try this recipe for perfect fluffy brown rice every time.

    1 cup brown rice
    2 cups water
    1 Tablespoon lemon juice

Put brown rice, water, and lemon juice into a pot and bring to a rapid boil over medium heat. Let rice boil rapidly for 5 minutes, uncovered (no lid), then turn heat down to a slow simmer and cover pot with a lid. Cook for 45 minutes or until all the liquid in the pot has been absorbed. Do not stir rice while it is cooking. The lemon juice in this recipe keeps the rice grains from clumping together. Lime or orange juice will do the same.

Hot Carob Milk

    2 cups soymilk
    3–4 Tablespoons honey
    ½ teaspoon vanilla extract
    2 Tablespoons carob powder, dark roasted

Put soymilk, honey, vanilla, and carob powder in the blender and blend until smooth. Pour mixture into a small pot and heat drink over medium heat. Stir to keep from scorching. Pour into a mug and enjoy!

Cinnamon Substitute

> 1 Tablespoon coriander, ground
> 1 Tablespoon cardamom, ground
> 1 teaspoon nutmeg, ground

Mix all ingredients together and use in place of cinnamon in any recipe.

Store cinnamon substitute in a jar or container.

Mock Parmesan Cheese Substitute

> ½ cup sesame seeds
> 2 Tablespoons nutritional yeast flakes
> 1 teaspoon salt

Put all ingredients into the blender and quick blend, just enough to break up the sesame seeds. Store in a container in the refrigerator.

Use as you would Parmesan cheese.

Yellow Colored Pasta or Rice

Pasta or rice can be colored yellow to give it cosmetic appeal for certain dishes where more color is desired. Simply add a couple of dashes of turmeric powder to the cooking water. Add turmeric a litttle at a time until the desired color is achieved. The pasta or rice will trun a bright sunshine yellow.

Super Air Popped Popcorn

Air pop a desired amount of popcorn in an electric air popper. Lightly mist with extra virgin olive oil and toss, then sprinkle on to taste: nutritional yeast flakes and sea salt. Garlic powder and onion powder can be used too. **Delicious!**

Honey Spice Toast

Toast a slice of bread. While bread is still hot, spread with a thin layer of honey. Top with a sprinkle of **Cinnamon Substitute**, (*see recipe, p. 132*). **Enjoy!**

Easy Garlic Toast

Spread a very thin layer of tahini on a slice of bread (not toasted), then sprinkle on garlic powder lightly, and a dash of salt. Place bread in the toaster or toaster oven at a low setting and lightly crisp bread.

Dad's Peanut Butter Banana Mud Slide

This is my Dad's own self-created concoction. He ate so much of it that he hasn't had it again to this day!

Lightly toast a rice cake in a toaster or toaster oven, be careful not to burn it. Spread toasted rice cake thickly with peanut butter. Place sliced banana on top of peanut butter and cover sliced banana with chilled **Carob Pudding**, (*See recipe, p. 117*). Sprinkle some shredded unsweetened coconut on top as garnish, and then enjoy!

Homemade Play Dough for Kids

    4 cups all purpose white flour
    4 cups water
    6 teaspoons cream of tartar
    1 cup salt
    ¼ cup vegetable oil

Put all ingredients into a large pot; stir until mixture is smooth and creamy. Cook on the stove over medium heat while stirring constantly until mixture becomes a dough. Remove dough from the pot and let cool before handling. Divide dough into pieces and color with food coloring. **Enjoy and Have Fun!**

THE NATURAL FOODS
PANTRY & SHOPPING LIST

This is a list of basic items you will need to make the recipes in this cook book. You may need additional items for special recipes that might be included in your weekly menu, or there may be items you would like to add to this list. These main stock items should be replaced as they are used up to keep your pantry stock replenished.

MAIN STOCK PANTRY ITEMS

Can Items

Tomato paste
Tomato sauce
Can beans—kidney beans, chickpeas or garbanzo beans, black beans, etc.
Can corn
Can fruit—peaches, pears, mixed fruit (Get can fruit without sugar added)
Coconut milk, premium
Sesame tahini
Black olives

Boxed Items

Assorted dry whole grain pasta—spaghetti, shells, noodles, elbows, etc.
Boxed whole grain dry or hot cereals
Soy milk

Bulk Foods

Whole wheat flour
Gluten flour or vital wheat gluten
Whole wheat pastry flour

Yeast (refrigerate)
Cornmeal
Oats
Flax seed
Walnuts
Cashews, raw
Brown rice
Bulgur wheat
Coconut (unsweetened, shredded)
TVP® (texturized vegetable protein)
Raisins
Nutritional yeast flakes
Agar agar

Bottled Items

Lemon juice
Fruit preserves (no sugar added)
Peanut butter or other nut butters
Honey
Pimientos
Bragg's liquid aminos
Extra-virgin olive oil, cold pressed organic

Herbs, Seasonings, & Extracts

Basil
Parsley flakes
Oregano
Onion powder
Garlic powder
Onion flakes
Garlic flakes
Sea salt
Paprika
Cayenne pepper
Turmeric
Thyme
Italian seasoning

Seitenbacher vegetable broth powder
Herbamare salt seasoning (Bioforce)
Vanilla extract (pure, non-alcohol)
Lemon extract
Almond extract
Ground coriander seed
Ground cardamom seed

MAIN STOCK REFRIGERATOR ITEMS

Tofu
Cucumber
Lettuce
Sprouts

Fresh produce items can be stocked according to refrigerator space and your fruit or vegetable preference. Buy what you need for the week if possible to prevent constant trips to the supermarket. Use up the most perishable produce items first.

Once opened, the following items will need to be refrigerated.

Soymilk
Lemon juice
Peanut butter
Tahini

All bulk foods should be kept refrigerated for longer storage.

MAIN STOCK FREEZER ITEMS

Frozen veggies- peas, broccoli. String beans, cauliflower, etc.
Tofu (Keep a cake of tofu frozen for special recipes)
Bread (Breads keep nicely in the freezer for long storage)

MAIN STOCK ITEMS THAT CAN BE LEFT OUT

Fresh tomatoes
Potatoes
Onions
Bananas

NATURAL FOODS GLOSSARY

Bragg's Liquid Aminos

Bragg's Liquid Aminos is derived from soybeans and is a great healthy alternative to soy and tamari sauce. It can be used to season protein dishes, cooked grains, and vegetables. Bragg's Liquid Aminos is not fermented and does not contain any alcohol, preservatives, additives, coloring agents, or chemicals.

Carob Powder

Carob powder is a wonderful alternative to chocolate. It can be used in cookies, pies, puddings, etc. Carob powder can be purchased raw or roasted; the roasted variety has a deeper flavor than the raw. Carob powder can be purchased at a health food store.

Cashew Nuts

The cashew nut grows at the end of a tropical pear shaped fruit called the cashew apple. Use raw cashews, not the roasted for cooking purposes. Cashews make an excellent base for non-dairy gravies, dressings, sauces, and other vegan recipes. Raw cashews should be frozen or refrigerated for long storage. Raw cashews can be purchased at a health food store.

Culinary Herbs

Herbs like basil, oregano, marjoram; parsley, etc. can be used to flavor and season various food dishes. Culinary herbs can be purchased fresh or dried. Fresh herbs have a livelier distinct flavor, while the dry herbs are more concentrated in flavor, convenient,and are preferred over the fresh for some recipes. Organic non-irradiated herbs are ideal.

Extracts

Extracts like almond, vanilla, or lemon extract should be alcohol-free. You can purchase alcohol-free extracts at your local health food store.

Sea Salt

Sea salt is derived from the ocean and is a healthy, nutritious salt alternative. Wet sea salt is different from the dry. Wet sea salt is unrefined, damp, not heat treated, and does not contain any chemical drying agents. Most dry sea salts contain chemical drying agents to keep the salt dry and free flowing. Lima French Atlantic sea salt is one brand of wet salt that can be used for cooking or baking and can be purchased at a health food store.

Soymilk

Soymilk comes from the soybean and is a wonderful alternative to dairy milk. Soymilk can be used for baking, cooking, pouring over cereal, or for pleasure drinking. Eden Soy Original is an excellent brand of soymilk, it is great tasting and creamy. It is lactose free and is high in calcium and protein. Edensoy can be used cup for cup in place of dairy milk in any recipe. There are many other brands of soymilk you can try; you can even make your own soymilk. Other dairy milk alternatives include almond milk, oat milk, and rice milk.

Sweeteners

Recipes can be sweetened without sugar using healthy alternatives like: honey, fruit juice concentrates, date sugar, applesauce, or dried fruit. Choose sweetener according to your preferred taste and the recipe need.

Tahini

Tahini is a creamy puree made from sesame seeds; it makes a great natural fat alternative to oil, butter, shortening, or margarine. Tahini can be used in baking, for cooking, or for browning tofu and some vegetables. Tahini is a whole food fat and is water soluble, which means it is an easy fat for the body's digestive juices to break down. JoYva sesame tahini is a good brand for cooking or baking, it is smooth, creamy, and thin in consistency. Raw tahini is also available.

Tofu

Tofu is the curd from coagulated soymilk. It is high in protein and calcium, in fact three ounces of extra firm tofu contains approximately 8-10 grams of protein. Tofu is bland in taste, but because of its porous texture it is able to soak up any flavor it is marinated in or seasoned with. Tofu serves as a protein base for burgers, dressings, ice cream, puddings, sauces, etc. Tofu is sold in four different textures: silken, soft, firm, and extra firm. The silken and soft textures are good for puddings, dressing, sauces, or scrambled tofu and tofu cheesecake. The firm and extra firm textures are good for slicing, cubing, baking, browning, grilling, or for use in various protein dishes. Tofu comes packaged in water, once opened the water should be drained off. Any leftover tofu should be stored in an air tight container and be covered with water one half inch over the top of the tofu and kept refrigerated. The water will need to be changed every other day to keep tofu fresh. Tofu can also be frozen to change its texture from a soft cottage cheese-like texture to a chewy spongy texture. The frozen texture of tofu is ideal for dishes where a meatier texture is desired. Once frozen, tofu cannot be blended or creamed.

TVP®

TVP® is texturized vegetable protein made from soy. TVP® is a meatless protein alternative and can be used in soups, casseroles, burgers, etc. It comes dry in the form of granules, chunks, strips, etc. and must be soaked in boiling water to rehydrate, and then you can flavor it and use it in any recipe as desired.

Whole Grains

Grains like rice, cornmeal, wheat flour, etc. should be purchased unrefined: meaning the whole grain is used- the bran, endosperm and the germ and no part is separated or removed. Whole grains are high in fiber and more nutritious. Whole grains are complex carbohydrates, which keep a stabilized blood sugar levels in the body. Breads, pasta, and other baked goods should be purchased made with whole grain ingredients.

INDEX

We'd love to have you download our catalog of titles we publish at:

www.TEACHServices.com

or write or email us your thoughts, reactions, or criticism about this or any other book we publish at:

TEACH Services, Inc.
254 Donovan Road
Brushton, NY 12916

info@TEACHServices.com

or you may call us at:

518/358-3494